# Kids 'N' Cops

# Kids 'N' Cops

◆

## Excerpts from Children's Letters, Artwork and Anecdotes

*Author: Joan Wellander-Kleppe*

iUniverse, Inc.
New York  Lincoln  Shanghai

# Kids 'N' Cops
## Excerpts from Children's Letters, Artwork and Anecdotes

iUniverse books may be ordered through booksellers or by contacting:

iUniverse
2021 Pine Lake Road, Suite 100
Lincoln, NE 68512
www.iuniverse.com
1-800-Authors (1-800-288-4677)

Front cover design by Mark Lipka, Artist

ISBN-13: 978-0-595-40048-5 (pbk)
ISBN-13: 978-0-595-84432-6 (ebk)
ISBN-10: 0-595-40048-5 (pbk)
ISBN-10: 0-595-84432-4 (ebk)

Printed in the United States of America

Dedicated
to
My precious children:
TOM, ALAN, BARBARA
for making life worthwhile
and ver-r-r-y interesting,

and

My precious grandchildren:
JOSH, JAKE, ZACH
HAYLEY, MORGAN
for adding sunshine and joy
to my life.

# Contents

# INTRODUCTION

*to*

*KIDS 'N' COPS*

The author, Joan Wellander-Kleppe, spent five years (1967-1972) as a Civil Service-appointed stenographer on the Commander's staff at the 19th (Town Hall) Chicago Police District. Her tasks included working with police personnel to implement the comprehensive free programs offered to youth in the community.

During that time period, the 19th District offered more opportunities for youth than any other district in the city. Police personnel and civilian volunteers coached and supervised the hundreds of boys who participated in the baseball, football, and the co-ed "Charlie, the Tuna" swim program.

Another effective and unique program initiated by District Commander John Fahey was the "Junior Patrol" membership aimed to educate elementary school-age boys about right and wrong. He believed that reaching youngsters at an early age was a crucial step in their becoming good adult citizens.

The author, with a background of education and experience in choral music, received the Department's blessing to found an a cappella choir for boys ages six to sixteen. This musical outlet was an activity that did not require equipment, nor the ability to read music, nor the physical ability to play sports.

For teen-age boys, the Explorers Post of the Law Enforcement Career Program offered more mature activities, such as assistance with the sports programs and the holiday "Wake-Break" service (free coffee to motorists).

During the school year, the Officer Friendly program was popular and effective.

Two patrolmen were appointed to visit all of the public and private schools in the District: one to cover the first-through-fourth grades, and the other to visit the fifth-through-eighth grades.

# THE MEN BEHIND THE BADGE

who validated their innate love of children.

- SUPERINTENDENTS: James B. Conlisk, Jr., Samuel Nolan, James Rochford;

- DEPUTY CHIEF: Robert Lynsky;

- CAPTAINS: Callahan, Fahey, Gannon, Lennon, Maurovich, Michaelsen, Scott, Smith;

- LIEUTENANTS: Gollogly, Krueger, Moriarty, Panek, Rothstein;

- SERGEANTS: Bullerman, Dockery, Gegner, Kleppe, McDermott, Runyan, Sarnowski, Wojda;

- PATROL OFFICERS: Barileau, Basil, Cesario, Cyrek, Dworak, Girard, Herman, Hippenmeyer, Jasch, Kilbane, Koburi, Koertgen, Laarveld, Lang, Lawrence, McKenna, McNee, Moore, Morahan, Opfer, Pack, Pizza, Smiegel, South, Spiropoulos, Tansey, Thomas, Vetrano, Walters, Weingart, Zaranti;

- CADETS: Corsentino, Durr.

# FOREWORD

"I hung your picture on my bedroom wall. You are my very best friend. All policemen are my friends. Tell them that."

This is only one of many quotations taken from the thousands of letters written to a Chicago police officer affectionately known as Officer Friendly "Uncle George" whose 'beat' was the public and parochial elementary schools in the 19th ('Town Hall') Police District.

His animated presentations captured the hearts of his attentive young audiences—boys and girls, ages six to ten, in the first through fourth grades. It proved that children have an innate ability to recognize sincerity, and George was no phony.

It was my privilege, as a civilian stenographer assigned to the same District, to accompany him on some of his visits and to respond to the children's letters on his behalf. George entrusted those original letters to me for safekeeping.

I have held on to these letters for more than thirty years, a sort of 'buried treasure', in a box that carefully accompanied me wherever I moved. After leaving the employ of the police department, my life took a detour into the corporate world. In the interim, 'Uncle George' passed away. It has been my long-suffering desire to honor his memory by publishing these gems of youthful wisdom in book form.

This may be the first published collection of 'billets-doux' received by a metropolitan police officer, hopefully to find a place alongside such children's musings as 'letters to God' and 'letters to Santa' that have entertained radio and television audiences. To retain their authenticity, none of the excerpts were edited as to spelling or grammar.

It is a precious record of children's curiosities, their need for a male role model and someone they could trust, their need for love and approbation, and promises made to do good.

# *PREFACE*

Few civilians have the opportunity to work behind the scenes as I did, to view police officers as ordinary people making extraordinary efforts in their commitment to serve and protect the public. From the moment I entered the halls of that landmark facility known as "Town Hall", my life and that of my children were forever happily changed—as were the lives of hundreds of children in that era.

Most citizens meet a police officer under a negative umbrella after doing something wrong, putting themselves on the defensive. To magnify the negativity of the situation, the attending officer may be having a 'bad' day, coming off as having an attitude. Understandably so. After all, they are humans, not robots. Their own personal stress—be it marital strife, illness, or financial problems—may seep into the performance of their duties.

There are few vocations with a built-in emotional elevator of up's and down's that police officers must face during every tour of duty. Of all the calls they respond to—a gang fight, a drug bust, a missing person, a dog bite victim, a lost child—the two most unpredictable and dangerous ones are what you might consider innocuous situations: 'domestic disturbance' and 'routine' traffic stop.

Frequently, in the case of domestic disturbances, the combatants pair up and attack the mediator—making a victim of the responding officer.

As to the routine traffic stop, I recall what happened to a rookie on his first day on the street. He stopped a motorist for a minor infraction of the law, never expecting a life-threatening reaction. As the driver lowered his window, he put a gun to the rookie's face and pulled the trigger—not once, but twice, in rapid succession. The gun miraculously jammed both times, but that dramatic close call motivated the officer to resign and seek a quiet desk job at a bank.

At the end of each tour of duty, police officers put the bad experiences behind them and replace them with the memory of a child's smile or wave because, behind every badge, beats a caring heart for children. I observed many tender moments during those years reminiscent of the Norman Rockwell portrait of a policeman sharing an ice cream moment with a young child.

Working behind the scenes, so to speak, getting to know and love the 350 police personnel assigned at the 19th District gave me an undiluted, realistic sense of the life and death, good and evil incidents they must cope with every day. It may be good to remember that when you see the familiar flashing lights in your rear view mirror coming up behind you.

# NOTES FROM THE AUTHOR

The year 1967 was filled with life-changing experiences for me. It began under the dark cloud of my mother's passing, the first death in my immediate family—a traumatic event forever burned in the fabric of my soul.

Then, the civic organization where I was employed lost its funding, leaving me to find employment with a regular paycheck in order to support my three minor children.

The Commander of the local police district, a board member of the strapped organization, suggested I take a Civil Service exam to qualify for a clerical position opening on his staff. I passed the exam with flying colors. Things were looking up! I was notified that I could start the job the following week, two days before Christmas. That was the same day my children and I became the owners of our first dog: a six-week-old puppy, a gift from a friend, a beautiful taffy-colored, sleepy-eyed, soft, cuddly, Shepherd-mix bundle of love that we named "Heidi".

None of us slept on that memorable eve, December 23. My children encircled the puppy as they spent the night on the living-room floor. I went to bed as a happy Mom, knowing how contented my children felt. The year that had begun so sadly seemed to be ending on an indescribably happy note.

I stayed awake for most of the night, feeling happy but a little apprehensive about starting a new job in the morning in an unfamiliar environment—a police station!

The thought of entering that formidable-looking, red brick two-story landmark was a little frightening. I had a flashback of being in that building once before, ten years earlier, when I timidly secreted myself at the rear of the second-floor courtroom. It was a surreal experience then to see my estranged husband, the father of my children, brought before a judge to be convicted of assault and battery against his unlikely paramour. I could never have imagined that someday I would be working in that very building.

As I climbed the stairs to the second floor, I breathed a happy sigh to see that the courtroom was gone. That big room was now filled with lockers for storage of the police officers' belongings. I could not imagine that the next five years would be one of the most interesting and happiest chapters of my life. There was nothing to compare it with because no other job offered such a change of scenery from day to day, nor such happiness and satisfaction.

Of all the programs offered to the citizenry, I believe the Officer Friendly program was the best public relations tool ever introduced by the Department and the one in which I was the most closely involved.

It brought a positive image of law enforcement into many homes, an image for personnel to aspire to. I viewed it as a sad day when it was subsequently discontinued, never to know what a difference it may have made in the thousands of lives that were touched.

It makes me wonder if the programs of the 60's and 70's would be as enthusiastically received in the 21$^{st}$ century as they were back then. The avenues of temptation have widened. People are jaded by the violence in movies and video games as well as graphic news coverage. Family ties are being tested by the need of both parents having jobs, assuaging their feelings of guilt for putting their children in day care by giving them material gifts as a substitute of personal 'quality' time, as the expression goes.

It is a different world than what we took for granted thirty years ago. We never heard the word 'terrorist', steroid use, celebrity rehabilitation, anger management therapy, postpartum depression, pedophiles, child abuse, intentional premarital pregnancies, foul language on radio and television, web site and television program blockers. Even the news programs expose us to graphic horror and indecency.

It is said that crime doesn't pay. It is crime *stopping* that doesn't pay. Many law enforcement officers still have to work a second job to keep up with the cost of living as they did years ago. I recall one officer who always came and went, in and out of the station, cheerfully singing. I thought he was just plain happy. I learned that, besides providing for his large family, he had a child with special needs. His musical eruptions were actually 'rehearsals' for his moonlighting job: a singing waiter at the elite Palmer House dining-room in downtown Chicago.

# LIFE IN THE POLICE STATION

## *(As I saw it)*

The environment of a metropolitan police station was not the rowdy, rough-talking place I had envisioned, nor was it the bustling, romance-laden venue portrayed in some television series programs. The officers never used foul language around me and never disrespected me in any way. They treated me and my children as part of the 'family'.

Late one afternoon at the station, extremely painful lower-back pains forced me to go home. When I realized the need to go to a hospital but without money to call a taxicab, I called the station for help. A squadrol was sent to pick me up but, en route, the squadrol was dispatched to an official call on my block. They enlisted the help of a fire department ambulance to transport me to a hospital.

Meanwhile, 'back at the ranch', the Vice squad checked with the squadrol for an update, assuming the wagon men had picked me up. The wagon men radioed back, "Oh, that was a DOA". The Vice men panicked, "Oh, no, not Joan! Now who's going to type our reports?" When I returned to work after painfully passing a kidney stone that fateful night, I teased them about keeping their priorities straight.

They helped to make one of my happiest Christmases ever—one that began quite disastrously. The night before Christmas Eve, my young daughter and I took a walk to the local butcher with our little Red Flyer wagon in tow. We put the few packages of meat in the wagon and proceeded to the corner grocery store for the Christmas dinner trimmings. Because of the cold weather, I brought my daughter inside. When we came out, the wagon was gone. I was not only heartbroken; I was 'broke', period. The next morning when one of the Vice men called to wish us a Merry Christmas, I blurted out what had happened the night before.

A few hours later, as my children and I were cleaning house, our front door-bell rang. There stood the three *'Wise' (Vice) Men* who handed me negotiable 'gold, frankincense, and myrrh' in the form of three $100 bills! Talk about happy endings!

The 'men in blue', whom I knew, had hearts of gold. They knew that I, a single parent and a lowly-paid civilian employee, really appreciated their kindnesses. About once month, they would set up reservations for my children and me to dine carte blanche at an upscale restaurant. We had a standing request with a neighboring family to borrow their son's sport coats for my sons' compliance to dress codes.

Amidst the ever-present pathos of crime and corruption encountered by these law enforcement officers, they usually sought a nugget of humor in every situation in order to cope with it rationally. This brings to mind an incident involving multiple calls at the same address involving a man threatening to jump from the second-floor roof. The Tactical team that responded was prepared to act but, instead, called his bluff with "Go ahead, jump". The 'jumper' indignantly shouted, "You want me to kill myself?"—followed by his swift retreat into the building and down to the street to submit to the arrest.

As I updated the station's personnel roster, I was amused by some of the names: there was a *John Lennon*, a *Pizza* with *Basil*, a *Black* and a *White*, a crossing officer with an apparent weathered face that looked like tanned leather whose first name was *Shirley*.

Some had nicknames like *'Harry, the Hip'*; *'Chicken Charlie'* or *'Chicken Feathers Charlie'* because he worked security at the poultry processing plant within the District's boundaries; and the District Commander himself was referred to as *'Father'* because of his extensive seminary education before joining the police department and still continued teaching Christian doctrine to teen-agers on Saturdays.

My three children loved the police officers as their new friends and role models. My daughter was thrilled to have a ride from our Warrant Officer who picked her up after grade school hours and brought her to 'my office'. Occasionally, she and I were chosen as a 'surveillance team' to check out gambling activity that the Vice Squad suspected might be emanating from a restaurant or beauty salon.

My two teen-age sons, who had concession-stand jobs along the lakefront, occasionally got high-speed rides via Tactical Team members from home to work. The siren and flashing lights treatment trimmed their 30-minute travel time by bicycle down to about four and one-half minutes. How many kids can boast that kind of experience!

One of the Desk sergeants had an alcohol-related problem. He sat on a stool with a swivel seat, once resulting in his sliding off as he turned too quickly. His perch put him above the high countertop so that a little old lady, coming in to ask a question, had to raise her head to talk to him. As he spoke down to her, she immediately began fanning the fumes from her face.

I personally observed the look on a citizen's face as he tried to report a crime and was advised, "Why don't you go home and call the police?!" The man's expression seemed to take stock of where he was: *I thought I WAS in a police station.*

During the riots of '68, all the squad cars, except two, were sent to help quell the disturbances. No one could believe these two remaining cars accidentally ran into each other! One of the supervisors quipped, "I can't wait to read the accountability report."

One of the versatile sergeants kept a basic woman's wardrobe at the station which he used for undercover work whenever there was a need to catch a serial offender who beat up on women. He could also pull off a character disguise as a drunk to attract assailants preying on inebriated patrons walking in a dark area. His talents belied his lovable, good-natured personality. His real specialty was being able to pick any lock, and he could double you over in laughter with his animated, funny story telling.

There were sad stories, too, of personal tragedies that many of these men had to deal with, yet still having to be rational and level-headed while serving the public. Just a few of the stories surfaced that touched our hearts. I couldn't imagine the heartbreak suffered by one of the most conscientious, older, pleasant officers whose son committed suicide at home, asphyxiated in a running car in a closed garage. One young policeman never recovered from depression of guilt after accidentally killing a young woman crossing the street as he answered an emergency call. He was exonerated, but he couldn't live with the memory.

One of the tallest young men on the Tactical Team was assigned to a detail where there was known drug trafficking. He approached a vehicle in a 'no parking' zone. When the occupant rolled down the window but refused to exit the vehicle, the soft-spoken officer did the unpredictable. He reached in and pulled the suspect right out through the window, bruising nothing but his ego.

One sergeant made it his mission to protect the well-being of youngsters who were found in the company of their parents in taverns. He would ask them to leave and suggest that *'next time, take your kid out for an ice cream cone instead.'*

The same sergeant was honored as "Police Officer of the Month" by WGN-TV and received a Department Commendation for exceptional humanitarian service: While on routine patrol of streets in the industrial area of the District, a citizen waved him down. The man hysterically related that a co-worker's fingers had been accidentally severed by a machine.

The sergeant radioed for an ambulance to pick up the wounded employee, then rushed into the building to ask the office girls to give him some ice cubes in a plastic bag in which to place that employee's severed fingers. As one girl fainted, another girl kept her wits about her and came up with an ice pack. As the ambulance transported the man to the hospital, the sergeant arrived there with the iced fingers. Thanks to the sergeant's quick thinking and action, and hours of micro surgery, the reattached fingers were saved and soon functional.

I proudly admit the above-noted sergeant was my husband. At the time, we were second-time-around newlyweds, living in a house we bought in the northwest section of the District. An interesting aside is that we unknowingly purchased it from a retired legendary police officer, Lieutenant Charles Fitzgerald, a 'Colombo'-type loner, who had solved some high-profile murder cases and for whom my husband had worked in years past.

We had lived in that neighborhood for about a month when a bizarre string of shootings were being attributed to a 'Sunshine Sniper'. He had been randomly shooting people in the early morning hours as they walked down the street in a shopping area only a few blocks from our house. In a bizarre turn of events, a lead emerged when a citizen approached the Field Lieutenant who was having a cup of coffee one morning at a restaurant counter and told him this puzzling story: he said his 'crazy' neighbor would shoot his van nearly every morning when it wouldn't start. In turn, the Lieutenant transmitted the information to my sergeant husband who had a hunch that the 'crazy neighbor' was demented enough to be the sniper. With the assistance of one of his best officers, he followed up on that possible lead.

Using descriptions of the vehicle and driver furnished by witnesses, and the address given by the van shooter's neighbor to the Field Lieutenant, the arrest was made at the sniper's residence as he was about to get into his bullet-ridden van.

And then there was George, a decorated patrolman before he became the endeared Officer Friendly "Uncle George" to the thousands of school children who came to know and love him.

He was the bridge of love that connected the children of the District with the police officers in the District and engendered respect for all figures of authority—parents and teachers, as well as all law enforcement figures.

Thus, the title, "Kids 'n' Cops"

# PROGRAMS FOR YOUTH

## CHICAGO'S 19ᵀᴴ POLICE DISTRICT'S

### BASEBALL and FOOTBALL

Hundreds of youth were involved in these sports programs. The overwhelming success could be attributed to the opportunity to rub shoulders with police personnel—to 'kick the dirt' on a level playing field. These were activities that most of the boys had never before experienced with a father figure, perhaps never even played 'catch' with one.

The uniforms and equipment were largely donated through grants received from insurance icon and generous philanthropist, W. Clement Stone. The Chicago Park District furnished the playing sites. Supervision and coordination came from hands-on participation by District personnel, and volunteers from civilian and professional life.

Local sports legends, Gayle Sayre and Ernie Banks, donated their time in special appearances and sports clinics.

### SWIMMING

This highly successful summer event called "Charlie, the Tuna", a name inspired by a television commercial, was open to boys and girls. Again, hundreds of neighborhood children enjoyed this free, supervised activity every day. At season's end, all received certificates of participation.

### JUNIOR PATROL

It was District Commander John Fahey's believe that reaching youngsters at an early age was a crucial step in their becoming good adult citizens. Toward that goal, he initiated the Junior Patrol program for elementary school-age children.

Each applicant was given a questionnaire to be completed, signed by a parent or guardian, and returned to the police station. Subsequently he would schedule a swearing-in ceremony at a local school to which the public as well as the child's parents would be invited to witness the event.

These occasions were emceed by members of the District's Youth Committee and officiated by local dignitaries:

Rev. George A. Rice, Department Chaplain/Youth
Committee Chairman
Commander John P. Fahey, 19th District, Chicago Police Department
Judge Kenneth Wendt, Presiding Judge, Narcotics Court
David O. Taylor, Personnel Director, WGN-TV
Alderman John Hoellen, 47th Ward
Alderman Joseph Kerwin, 46th Ward
State Representatives John Merlo and Art Telcser
Ed Kelly, Superintendent, Chicago Park District/48th
Ward Committeeman
George Mazarakos, Principal, Lane Technical High School

## JUNIOR PATROL A CAPPELLA CHOIR

What began as an experiment, became an overnight phenomenon. Commander Fahey allowed me to test my ethereal dream of founding an a cappella choir to give boys an opportunity to perform in an activity other than sports. Unlike forming a band, this would not require any equipment other than a voice.

The idea was put into motion. As the boys picked up a Junior Patrol application from the Commander, he would ask these budding Caruso's to sing for him—anything from the alphabet to Old MacDonald's Farm. In spite of driving his male secretaries crazy, he would then steer the little crooners to my office for an 'interview'.

This was the first of its kind in the Department, and, within two weeks of its formation, I had a roster of 90 boys between the ages of 6 and 16. Most of them could actually carry a tune!

## OFFICER FRIENDLY PROGRAM

Without a doubt, this was the best public relations tool ever employed by the Department. In each District, two patrolmen were appointed to visit all public and private schools—one for first-through-fourth grades, and the other for fifth-through-eighth grades. For many youngsters, these were the only male role models they could relate to.

The late Officer Friendly 'Uncle George' Zaranti creatively forged a trust, with the thousands of children he visited, through his obvious sincerity blended with a refreshing sense of humor. He subliminally filled the children's need for a father figure which apparently was lacking in many of the households. He brought a positive image of law enforcement into the homes. In effect, he became part of the family as attested to in the hundreds of letters he received every week. It was a sad day when the program was discontinued, never to know what a difference it made.

**Teens in the**
**EXPLORER POST**
**LAW ENFORCEMENT CAREER PROGRAM**
**kick off**
**"WAKE-BREAK" for holiday motorists**
**at the 1st District (headquarters)**

CITY OF CHICAGO / DEPARTMENT OF POLICE
Explorers Post
Law Enforcement Career Program
kick off "Wake-Break" 69
(free coffee for motorists) on
Memorial Day week-end,
in nation wide publicity,
north side represented
by: Tom Wellander
for the 19th District

# MEET 'UNCLE GEORGE' ZARANTI

### _The Cop "Framed" by 12,832 Children_

Officer Friendly George Zaranti's was assigned to visit all of the public and private elementary schools in the 19th Police District. He was allowed to construct whatever approach he thought would be appropriate and effective in gaining the attention and confidence of the first-through-fourth grade boys and girls. The response was magnetic: they not only listened; they besieged him for his photo to take home and frame.

Wherever he went, the adulation was the same. Chicago Police Headquarters' Neighborhood Relations division never expected the ever-mounting popularity of a single police officer to cause a huge backlog of requests for his photo. They had never witnessed his charismatic connection with the youngsters. It was phenomenal.

In effect, he became part of all these children's families—a sort of surrogate uncle.

"Uncle George" embodied a bigger-than-life image that had the positive impact on the public that was needed at a time when public opinion of law enforcement personnel had ebbed, and the use of drugs and disrespect of authority had escalated.

It was soon obvious that District Commander Fahey had appointed the right person for this liaison job. I remember that day. George was excited. He telephoned his mother from the Commander's office: "Mamma, Mamma (continuing in Italian to tell her the good news.)" His Mamma cried with pride and joy to hear that her Georgie had become somebody 'importante'.

His assignment covered 27 schools with 404 classrooms which translated into 12,832 students in his first round of visits. He received at least that many letters from the children, gathered by the teachers or individually mailed to him. Every day, after his tour of duty, he would sit down with me to read the letters and make suggestions as to anything special that I should include in the response. He giggled like a school boy the day he received his first kiss on the cheek.

It was an enjoyable, memorable opportunity when I got to accompany him on a visit to a school and witness firsthand the students' adulations. They were enchanted by his animated presentations. A flood of fan letters addressed to him followed every visit—each one filled with love and appreciation for what he had taught them, and, without fail, a request for his photo.

He personally autographed each 8" x10" photo along with the words, "I love you, dearly." In his reply he told the children to stand the photo on their dresser as a reminder to 'be good, don't smoke, and never hurt anybody."

He became well-known beyond the 19th District boundaries, beyond the city limits, throughout Illinois. Other patrol officers admitted that, in the midst of making a "bust", an arrestee would ask, "Do you know Uncle George?" Occasionally, someone on the street would yell to an officer in a squad car, "Hey, are you Officer Friendly?"

His presentations were punctuated with humor and accompanying body language which amused the teachers as well as the students. He called his comical movements the "Sicilian Watusi" or the "La Cucaracha Conga". He referred to the girls and boys as "Honeys, Friskies, and Peter Rabbits" and confessed that their expressions of love and laughter made him "feel good all over." They came up with affectionate nicknames for him, too: Tarzan, Superman, a panda, a Saint Bernard puppy, a big teddy bear, and Santa Claus.

For starters, he asked the children to guess what he always carried with him. Of course, the logical answer was 'gun'. "No," he said, "a toothbrush!" and then would pull a toothbrush out of his holster. He teased, "Do you know who likes you?" His answer was, "7-Up…it says so on the bottle." He referred to himself as a 'meatball' because of his Sicilian heritage.

If the children were in the playground when he arrived at a school, they could tell it was he because of the 'smiley face' painted on the front of his yellow VW bug auto.

Before Christmas, he played Santa Claus in full costume at the police station. The line of children would be a block long the whole day. George would not get back his normal voice for a week.

He involved himself in helping with the station's other programs organized by police personnel targeted for youths of the District: 'Charlie, the Tuna' swim program, 'touch' football and baseball activities. Occasionally, he had time to visit the boys' choir that I had started, at rehearsals or performances, but he didn't have to be told that singing was not his forte.

Reading the excerpts from the children's letters, you got the feeling that there was only ONE, REAL, Officer Friendly in the world: "Uncle George." They bared their thoughts, feelings, and fears with the honest innocence that only children can express.

These are some of the subjects he used to start discussions with them:

> What colors are the checkerboard bands on police officers' hats?
> What do we say about guns? About drugs?
> What number do you call when you see something wrong?
> How many ways do you look when you cross the street?

He asked the children to put their hands on their hearts and promise:

> "I promise never to take candy, ice cream, Barbie dolls. Thumbelina dolls, bicycles, kitty cats, little birdies, or anything else, unless I have permission from my Mommy and Daddy."

# THE COP KIDS LOVED

# PATROLMAN "UNCLE" GEORGE ZARANTI

### *The Cop Kids Loved*

Officer Zaranti's bigger-than-life image had the positive impact on the public that was needed at a time when public opinion had ebbed in the late 60's, and the use of drugs was escalating. It was soon obvious that the right person had been appointed for the District's "Officer Friendly". I remember that day. George was excited. He called his mother, "Mamma, Mamma" (he went on in Italian to tell her the good news. "Mamma" cried with pride and joy.)

His first round of visits to 1$^{st}$-through-4$^{th}$ grade students involved 27 schools, 404 schoolrooms—for a total of 12,832 boys and girls, all of whom received an 8" x10" black-and-white photo of George (happily furnished by Headquarters) inscribed, "I love you dearly, Uncle George."

**Three first graders in red, green, and yellow dresses help Officer Friendly in instructing students about the meaning of traffic signals.**

It is all seriousness as the children learn about Stranger Danger.

**19th District**
**OFFICERS FRIENDLY**
**ZARANTI and SPIROPOULOS**
reading school children's letters

# LET THE LETTERS BEGIN!

◆　　◆　　◆

Your like a second father to me because you don't only act like an uncle but you also act like a father. You even remind me of him when your in Room 201, and he sometimes reminds me of you.—Love, Carmen

◆　　◆　　◆

My mother and father think you are very nice and comical with children the way I describe you, and I think so too. They want me to send a letter to the Sun-Times about you.

◆　　◆　　◆

I want to tell you something that happened to us with a firecracker. One day, my family went riding on a busy street when two boys put a firecracker in the middle of the street. My father had to move into another lane. Would our car blow up if my father went on top of the firecracker? Please answer this question. Truly your Italian meatball.—Anna

◆　　◆　　◆

When we were talking about nationalities, you said your father was born in Sicily. My grandparents were born there too.—Kathy

♦      ♦      ♦

I like you for a father. I hope you be on TV. Take care of yourself.—Humberto

♦      ♦      ♦

I told my Mom about you. She said you was a bg help to the public. My mom said give him a complinest when you see him.—Lisa

♦      ♦      ♦

*A TEACHER INCLUDED THIS NOTE WITH A BATCH OF LETTERS*

*he children wanted to write you letters and invite you to see their costumes or Halloween. Hope you can understand their spelling. They spell the way it sounds to them. Enjoy them. I think they're cute.—Ellen*

I like you for a father. If only you were my teacher. I hope you will live a long long time. Take care of yourself.—Lupe

♦      ♦      ♦

I wish you lived next door so I could visit you every day. I want to be just like you when I grow up.—Jose

♦      ♦      ♦

By my house there are gangs who are breaking the factory windows and the doors of the factory. And now they are breaking windows in our house. They are throwing rocks at the car windows and taking the tires off the cars. They put beer cans in the cars, then they go on the railroad tracks and stand there drinking beer. Our world is funny today.—Joseph

◆     ◆     ◆

The lady next door was sweeping her porch and a rat came on the porch, and it wouldn't get off. The Aristocrats (*Ed. Note: a local street gang*) broke the window in a carin a lot near our house. They set it on fire. When I was going to school Monday, one of my classmates and I went in the alley and there we saw something that made us think someone might have been attacked.—Michael

◆     ◆     ◆

I obey you because if you didn't tell me about poisons, I could be dead right now.

◆     ◆     ◆

*(Ed. Note: Considering all these letters were written by first-through-fourth graders, their opinions and vocabulary are quite mature and insightful)*

◆     ◆     ◆

I like when you teach us about bad and good.—Angela

◆     ◆     ◆

I want to flunk so I can still see you next year. I hope you aren't board with my letter.—Vivian

◆     ◆     ◆

I hope you don't get hurt on the job. I love you as much as you love me.—Margaret

I hope you like these funny poems I found in a book:

> One bright day in the middle of the night,
> Two dead boys got up to fight.
> Back to back they faced each other,
> Drew their swords and shot each other.

> A deaf policeman heard the noise,
> Came and questioned the two dead boys.
> If you do not believe this lie is true,
> Ask the blind man, he saw it, too.

> *Come little book to me, and be my friend.*
> *I'll turn your pages, one, two, three,*
> *Until I reach the end.*

—Kelly Ann

◆    ◆    ◆

Thank you for showing us the bullet. Have a nice time and also take care.—James

◆    ◆    ◆

I love you just as much as my parent. Please come see my family some time. We will have a partty for you aspeasily.—James

◆    ◆    ◆

My whole family likes you. My cousin gots a picture of you. He said he would not go to bed without it. My little brother wants a picture of you but I don't know where to buy it at.—Julia

◆    ◆    ◆

I am going to be a real American, love my flag and country. I do not like people wearing my flag for trousers.—Jelena

◆     ◆     ◆

You don't know how I miss you. I think you are one of the best policeman on the force. I think when you are around, you make everyone happy.—Roberto

◆     ◆     ◆

You are the funest offer I have ever seen. I have never shook a policeman's hand before. I wish you would be my father. I will look at your pitcher every time I go to my bedroom to remember you.—Julie

◆     ◆     ◆

I like police very much. They help me, and I help them. They do their duty, and we help them do it by telling if your friend does something wrong.—Robert

◆     ◆     ◆

Our teacher tells us to bring pages from the newspaper about people who use dope. The stories are sad. Boys and girls are silly to take dope. I am never going to do that.—Robert

◆     ◆     ◆

I wish you won't go to a shooting where men fight when you have to go out for a alarm and get hurt and try not to put yourself in the hospital or get shot in the back by a killer. Try to get all the allful men that try to kill kids and kidnap mothers that take children away in their cars.—Cherrie

◆     ◆     ◆

You did not tell us about your gun. I saw a man, he got closer to me. Then I ran across the street.—Larry

◆    ◆    ◆

You are a very nice man because you help people when they need help and you know what to do with a gun. I know you don't have any children because your wife never had a baby and you want a child.—Peter

◆    ◆    ◆

I liked your jokes. They were funny. I liked it when you pretended to take two of my freckles.—Kelly

◆    ◆    ◆

Aver butty likes you. Even teacher likes you, but we all like you.—Tina

◆    ◆    ◆

I wish you would be my Daddy. I wish I was a police woman. If I do become a police woman, would you teach me?—Paulina

◆    ◆    ◆

When I was 2, my Mother died and I am said.—(unsigned)

◆    ◆    ◆

I love you very much and I wish I can live with you but I got my own parents to love.—Pamela

◆    ◆    ◆

I am happy you call me Peter Rabbit. Your so funny. Can I call you Peter Rabbit? You were rite when you said we have a lovely teacher.—Love, Carol

◆　　　◆　　　◆

I like it when you call us peter rabbits. WHY DO YOU CALL US PETER RABBITS?—Robert

◆　　　◆　　　◆

I am glad you are a policeman. You tell me funny stuff. Bring a can of meatballs when you come. You are so importend because you tell us about fires. DON'T CALL ME PETER RABBIT.—Karen

◆　　　◆　　　◆

How come people who take dope have to have it when they get older?—Frank

◆　　　◆　　　◆

Hi there, my name is Melody. Well here is 3 qustange:

1.  Why do I like you?　　　　_____

2.  Why do I care for you?　　　_____

3.  Where do you live?　　　　_____

Please write back on the lines I made for you.—Melody

◆　　　◆　　　◆

I love my parents, teacher, you and the firemen. I know a lot about dope: aspirns, alckeselzers, exerdin, Mommys medicine pills. My parents love me. They always holler when I do wrong because they love me.—Brenda

◆     ◆     ◆

I hope you are a policeman in till you are 65 years old or longer.—Love, Georgiann

◆     ◆     ◆

Every time I go trick and treating, I always ownly go by my friends houses. You taught me a lot—Karen

◆     ◆     ◆

When I was in kindergarten, I hardly knew anything about drugs. But ever since you kept coming in, I learn more every year.—Chester

◆     ◆     ◆

I will never take medicine unless I'm sick, and I will never listen to people who say that they will drive me home or say that they will give me a bike. I will always check the candy I get from Halloween.—Richard

◆     ◆     ◆

*(Ed. Note: Because of a notorious case at the time of Officer Friendly's visit to the schools wherein a pedophile offered a bicycle to lure boys to his apartment to pose for pornographic material, 'Uncle George' included that item in the promise he asked children to make.)*

◆     ◆     ◆

I never learned to run across the street. I promise never to take no candy from nobuty.—Donna

◆      ◆      ◆

You make learning fun.—Randa

◆      ◆      ◆

I wish you was my teddy bear to love and hug. Will you send me a police hat, please?—From your Peter rabbit, Edwardo

◆      ◆      ◆

I love you just as much as I love God. Every day I think of you. If I ever broc up with you, I wude cry.—Love, F.

◆      ◆      ◆

*(Ed. Note: A third-grade teacher wrote this note to George: I really appreciate your coming over. The kids just love you–they really do.—Miss Luci*

We made Christmas things, a Santa, a rain deer, an angle, a star, and a bell. I like Christmas, do you?—Corrine

◆　　　◆　　　◆

I am sending 3 pictures of me, one for you, one for your captain, and one for your wife.—Scott

◆　　　◆　　　◆

Will you send me a picture of you and some other police in their unit? I'll never forget you and the others as long as I live.—Patricia

◆　　　◆　　　◆

You know what? One day in fall we were playing a game, and a drunk came along so we started to run because we thought that he mite hurt us. We ran real fast through my yard, and when we came back, he was gone. So we started to play, and he came past every day then for a couple of days. Then he went away and never came back.—Jimmie

◆　　　◆　　　◆

You are a funny guy, and I like your jokes and jigs.—Herbert

◆　　　◆　　　◆

My cat got run over on Saturday morning. I want to get a new cat but my father said that I can't get one. My cat had a kitten and the kitten looks all around for her. But I know we are not to talk about cats, but that is all I can think about. But I can think you are good.—Aydie

◆     ◆     ◆

*(Ed. Note: A teacher wrote: My third-grade class is studying Chicago and, because of our lesson, we would appreciate it if you would let us come sometime to have a visit at the Town Hall police station. We are 35 in all. Thanks.)*

◆     ◆     ◆

I love you and all the police officers because they make it safe for children to go to school and home. It makes the people safer to know we have so many policemen to help fight for a safe city.—(Unsigned)

◆     ◆     ◆

*(Ed. Note: The following jokes were submitted by a boy named 'Gene' and the family housekeeper named "Martha" which appeared in a section called "Today's Chuckle", clipped from a local newspaper:*

*"The tourist had just arrived in California, delighted with the way his car had withstood the rigors of the trip. 'How were the roads?', he was asked. 'Well, this guy LINCOLN laid out a great highway, but that Frenchman DE TOUR was no road builder at all.'"*

◆     ◆     ◆

*Why was Adam the first electrical engineer? Because he supplied the connection for the first loud speaker: a WOMAN!*

◆     ◆     ◆

I hope the older children don't call you 'pig' or 'fuzz' because I think your nice.—Mary Lu

◆     ◆     ◆

I like you because you are nice and let me put on your handcuffs.—Ramon

◆     ◆     ◆

I liked the story about the boy that did all the stealing, and when he bit off his mother's nose.—James

◆     ◆     ◆

I will never rob anybody because I will go to jail.—Ruben

◆     ◆     ◆

Police are very good friends. They help people. They prevent crimes. You have to be smart to be a police.—Sandra

◆     ◆     ◆

I want to know if someone ever shot you in the leg. Also thank all the other policemen for helping Chicago and other lands.—Miriam

◆     ◆     ◆

I love you because you are funny and you teach us about bad things. We cannot take anything that is not ares. If it is are Mother or Father's, we cannot take it. I love you and I know you love me and more childrens. I love you.—Susan

♦         ♦         ♦

*(Ed. Note: Notice how the lack of spontaneity reduces reader's interest when a generic letter is put on the blackboard by the teacher for all the children to copy):*

*I like you because you are good to me. We all love you very much. I hope you like me too. I like you the best. Your dance is funny. I love you. I do not take dope.*

♦         ♦         ♦

We love you because you help us learn all about safety and all about the danger of taking medicine by ourself and about talking to strangers. You said that was very dangerous. We love you for all the things you taught us.—Pamela

♦         ♦         ♦

I hope you have a beautiful Christmas. I hope you don't have to shoot anybody.—Lisa

♦         ♦         ♦

I hope you have a happy Christmas and will not have to work hard. I hope you will not have to catch a robber or someone who stole a car, and if you do, I hope you will not slide on the ice. So be careful that you will not slide on the ice.—John

♦         ♦         ♦

## THE EDUCATION DIRECTOR OF THE CHICAGO BOYS CLUB WROTE:

*Thank you for donating your time at the career fair. Your presence contributed to the success of this event. The members, each in his own personal varied way, appreciated the efforts which you have made on their behalf.*

*At times, simply the opportunity of meeting someone in your profession is a thrill to boys and girls.*

♦　　♦　　♦

I wish you were really my uncle. My uncle past away. I mean he died.—Sandy

♦　　♦　　♦

I love you very much, and I think you are like WOW!—Lynnae

♦　　♦　　♦

We all wish that you become the chief of brave policemen. I will never forget you. At bedtime, I always say a prayer for you so you will not get hurt.—Carol

♦　　♦　　♦

*(Ed. Note: The following thank-you letter to 'Uncle George' was received from the Little Sisters of the Poor and the residents of St. Joseph Home for the Aged):*

*I join these dear people in their greetings to you, "Uncle George". I'm sure anyone who has given so much to others throughout the year will really have a blessed Christmas. We hope some time next year you will again come back to St. Joseph's. The audience is always new. Time has a way with the aged. Call me when you are ready.—Sister Virginia*

◆    ◆    ◆

You were very funny when you visited our classroom, but you got your message across: "Don't take drugs unless your mother or father says you can." I am proud of the Chicago Police Department and what they do for people.—Steve

◆    ◆    ◆

I like policemen and will try to do good, and eat meatballs.—Mary

◆    ◆    ◆

Every time I see a policeman, I will remember about Uncle George.—Albin

◆    ◆    ◆

I hung your picture on my bedroom wall. You are my very best friend. All policemen are my friends. Tell them that.—Louise

◆    ◆    ◆

I hope you do not kill anyone because that is sad for you. I hope you do not get hurt when you are a nice man. Have you ever read a book called "Winnie, the Pooh"? No, or yes.—Zolene

◆    ◆    ◆

I will never skip school until I'm threw with college.—Neil

◆     ◆     ◆

Please send me your picture. It would make a good picture in my wolit.—Horacio

◆     ◆     ◆

*(Ed. Note: Most of the letters are decipherable, but here's a puzzling one):*

My cousin she ate poison, and she did not say her parents, and she died, and baby sister got some of the medicine. My friend she was sick and she ate the wrong medicine, and this girl she see the man, and he said, 'Did you want some candy?' and it was poison, and this boy he was at his house and the man give him a apple and there was a sliver in it.—Nancy

◆     ◆     ◆

You look like Buddy Hackett. I like how you dance so does the girl that sits next to me.—Valerie

◆     ◆     ◆

Most of all we like you when you shake your but. You were so funny yesterday.—Darlene

◆     ◆     ◆

You said to me that I was cute and I had puppy dog pierced earrings and you said that when I get married, if you husband asked what I wanted, you said someone would call out a golden pair of earrings.—Lori

◆          ◆          ◆

Once you were sick or something, we had officer whats-his-face, and he wasn't funny at all. You are a nice policeman, even SUPER.—Audrey

◆          ◆          ◆

I am asking you a favor, would you please send me a box of junior police cards, and how much are the handcuffs?—Michael

◆          ◆          ◆

When I was little, I wanted to be many different things. Now I want to be a doctor. Here's a little joke: Roses are red, coal is black, so do me a favor and sit on a tack.—Ann Marie

◆          ◆          ◆

I hope you are capturing more bad guys to tell us about them.—Anne Judith

◆          ◆          ◆

*(Ed. Note: The following excerpt from a newspaper article was mailed to him anonymously:*

*He is short, thoroughly Sicilian, with the same bulldog smile and the meaty fists clopping heads of third graders like they were tender little cabbages.*

*George Zaranti, a good cop and a better Officer Friendly, is Chicago's greatest, loudest, most pugnacious officer representing "Chicago's Finest" every day, school after school. Every day, more kids are getting to know him, and many more kids getting turned on to his 'drugs are N.G.—No Good' routines. George only hopes that they'll remember what he told them.*

*He continues to crusade against medicines that look like candy. He would like to see drug manufacturers put a skull-and-crossed bones symbol on any medication that would be harmful to children, whether taken accidentally or purposely—a universal symbol easily recognized by anyone. He sees no compromise of any sort regarding drugs.*

*Children crowd for a place on his lap, write letters to him, and maul him in parking lots.*

◆        ◆        ◆

I hope you will come back soon because I love you and about 20,000 kids love you. You probably have a pretty wife because you are so handsome.—Tony

◆        ◆        ◆

You are the funniest man in the world. You are what people call hilarious.—Carlos

◆        ◆        ◆

I am thankful to you for showing us what is wrong and what is good.—Your little Mexican meatball.—Chuy

◆        ◆        ◆

I wish I could be a policeman just like you, and I want to tell you that I like meatballs, too.—Your little American friend, David

◆        ◆        ◆

I like all your police cars and your police boats.—Henry

◆     ◆     ◆

I will always remember you even when I die.—Laurie

◆     ◆     ◆

Some people put poison things in candy when children go out for Halloween, and some people try to give other people Dope. If one day they try to
give me some, I will say 'No thanks'.—Love, Lovita

◆     ◆     ◆

I'm glad that you came to our room to teach us not to eat drugs. Some people eat drugs that are crazy.—Sincerely yours, Kelly

◆     ◆     ◆

How are you? I am find, and I hope you are to. I want to know if you ever
had troble in a fright because I want to know. I would say that dop is bad,
but some of my friends take it. They told me that if I wanted to try it, and I
said 'if YOU want to take it, I will not, because you are just hurting yourself'. And please send a picture. I can't wait.—Good by, your friend, Allen.
(Write back please!)

◆     ◆     ◆

I think drugs are sickening. Nobody in my family took drugs. My mother
and father don't have a lot of medicine in our house. I don't have much to
say but would you send me a photograph, please?—Karen

◆     ◆     ◆

I like you very much. I hope you will come again. You taught me that dope
and pills are both poisons, and if you see medicine with your dad's name on
it, you cannot take it, and I want you to know that my uncle is a policeman
too.—Heidi

◆     ◆     ◆

Do you think that people are nuts to take drugs and steal to kill people for no reason and rape a person. I say that they are nuts to do things like that and they ought to be killed instead of gest getting out of jail and doing it again and then they get out again and then do it again and go to jail for life.—Paul

◆     ◆     ◆

How is it at the Police Office? I hope you will get all the robbers you need. I would like to be an F.B.I. when I grow up. I'll send you a Valentine some day.—Your fan, Kenneth

◆     ◆     ◆

We went to court to get a man into jail for breaking our front door window, but we had to drop charges because our witness disappeared because he is too chicken to appear in court. Our tenants in a different house had been burglarized by this man. Lots of annoying dangerous things happen around here, but we are still praying for a good neighborhood. We are not giving up.—Phillip

◆     ◆     ◆

The Aristocrats (*street gang*) tore up a drum yesterday. We don't have any gangs by my house, and we don't have any writing on the buildings. Are we lucky.—H. J.

◆     ◆     ◆

*(Ed. Note: The following letter from a 4 th Grader could be used as a one-paragraph seminar for high schoolers and adults!):*

Dear George: How are you? I hope OK. You should stop smoking, if you smoke, because it burns the liver and lung. I knew a man and he got a hole in his throat from smoking. Some people like to smoke grass, but grass is bad for your heart and blood pressure. It makes your heart beat faster and makes your blood pressure go up and could give you a heart attack. And it makes your mind wander, and later in time it makes your mind weak, and you cannot think fast, and it slows up your reflexes.—Kennith

◆　　◆　　◆

*(How about this direct approach):*

Do not take drugs. This is why:

1.　You will get sick.

2.　They are not good.

3.　They are bad for you.

4.　You might die.

5.　They will make you act crazy

Are you all right, George?—Deborah

◆　　◆　　◆

I try my best to listen to my pearntes and my lovely teacher, and when I get bigger I promise I will never take dope or smoke grass or take mairuana.—Love, Brenda
(P.S. right me back, ok, and try to send me a picture of you, ok. By now)

◆　　◆　　◆

I don't want to grow up taking drugs and destroy my life. I don't think you want to start taking drugs, do you? I like it very much when you come to visit us because you always teach us a good lesson about teenagers and drugs today, and it is wonderful to have an Officer like you to teach us that stuff. I wish that I knew how a police station looks and what kind of work you do there too. If you can write back, answer my questions at the top. My name is Laura, I live on the second floor, and I'm 8 years old.—P.S. PLEASE TRY TO WRITE BACK.

◆     ◆     ◆

Thank you for making me learning more each year. Now I know more about drugs.—Your meatball, Tom

◆     ◆     ◆

I want to know more about drug abuse. I wish you could come and talk to us about drugs. I watched a move called "Go Ask Alice'. It was about a girl who was on drugs. Please write soon. We miss you.—Jessica (P.S. I DIDN'T FORGET THE ITALIAN MEATBALLS.)

◆     ◆     ◆

Thank you for teaching us about medicine. All of us are glad that you teacyh us about medicine, or we could get sick and die from it. Thank you for coming to our class room. You mean very much to me. Uncle George, please send me a picture of you.—Sylvia

◆     ◆     ◆

I am Raquel and I go to Robert Morris School in room 309, and I want to thank you for going their and I also want to thank you for the picture and lesson and coloring book you gave me. You are very nice and funny. I promise you never to take drugs, like you told me, because I will go nuts. I hope to see you again. Write back soon.—Your friend Raquel who will never forget you. (P.S. Please I ask you, write back soon. Good by)

◆          ◆          ◆

*(Ed. Note: The Post Office delivered the following letter, even though the stamp was a Christmas seal!)*

I like you. You are funny, and I love you. My mother and father only take medicine, only when they are sick, and sometimes I have to take medicine, only with permission.—Love, Andrew

◆          ◆          ◆

I was glad to see you! I like the way you go PO5-1313 in that funny way. You are the best in teaching us about drugs. I like your baby, he is cute. How old is he? Please give me a picture the next time you come to are room.—Richard

◆          ◆          ◆

I am the one who told you about my brother 15 years old, remember? Do you have a telephone number so when anybody offers me dope, so I can call you. And, please, please, send me your handsome picture. I think you are so handsome. Oh, yes, I forgot. I am in room 206, Mr. McMahon's room. He is so nice to us. For a sample, he lets us have candy, but we cannot chew gum or eat sunflower seeds or them pixie stix either, or them hot tooth pix either. Mr. MacMahon likes Eloise and me, and I the best.—Christine (I love you.) (Please send your picture and your phone number if you have one.)

◆          ◆          ◆

I think you are the nices man I every met. I love you. May I have your picture?—Lori

◆　　◆　　◆

*(Ed. Note: The following letter was decorated with drawings of pills, a container of 'likwid' drugs, and skull-and-crossed bones)*

Do not eat drugs. Where do you get them? Just from your Mother, Father, and a doctor. And don't eat candy from stranger-danger. Will you please give me a pitcher of you? May I have your auditgrafe too?—Lynn

◆　　◆　　◆

How are you? Fine, I hope. Remember your last visit to Prescott School? It was very kind of you to come. I'll be in fifth grade next year, but I'll still remember you because you were so funny and nice. Oh, I almost forgot to tell you. Remember when you mentioned drugs? I remember that, and I promise I will never take them unless I have to.—Love, Teresa

◆　　◆　　◆

*(Ed. Note: George received the following query from the Jacksonville, Illinois School for the Deaf):*

*We are trying to get all plans made for the trip to Chicago. Will we be able to tour the police station, and can you attend the basketball game on Sunday afternoon?*

I love you very much. I love you. I like the way you tell us what is bad and what is good. I like policemen. I do not take anything from any bubbie.—Carol

◆　　　◆　　　◆

One time a burglar broke into our house and stold ten dollars.—Alan

◆　　　◆　　　◆

I have been a good boy. A good boy is not a bad boy. I know a cousin that plays whis maches. I love you very, very, very, very, very much.—Love, Rocky

◆　　　◆　　　◆

I went to camp and saw a deer, and I went boating and saw a shark, and that's all I have to say, and I'm your buddie, and I love you.—Mike

◆　　　◆　　　◆

You teached us a lot in school. We all love you. I will listen to what you say. One day we had a fire and I began to cry because our house burned down. I love my teachers too.—Love, Eddie

◆　　　◆　　　◆

Burglars are bad. Kids are good.—Mark (D.)

◆　　　◆　　　◆

In all my years I have never met a funnier man than you. It's nice to have a friend like you. I wish you luck and a good life through all your years.—Mark (M.)

◆　　　◆　　　◆

I want to tell you that a boy got hit by a car. That day you came to our class, you forgot to talk about fire. We are all to respect all rules. When we are playing outside, we have to watch bikes and cars. We are trying to be good citizens.—Love, Ivelisse

◆　　　◆　　　◆

Thank you to tell the dangerest and strangest medicine.—Arleen

◆　　　◆　　　◆

It is good our policemen our on there tose.—Faustino

◆　　　◆　　　◆

Did you put anyone in jail yet?—Yours greatful, Peter

◆　　　◆　　　◆

I know the police number. I will call you if I see big people fighting and little people fighting. Happiness is love.—Love, Cathy (P.S. Please write back to us)

◆    ◆    ◆

I wish to be like you when I grow up.—Hector

◆    ◆    ◆

*(Ed. Note: This boy covers all the bases!)*

I'm staying out of trouble in school and at home and at the park and in the zoo and in the store.—Your friend, Mark

◆    ◆    ◆

I'd like to go home with you. I'll ask my mother.—Peter

◆    ◆    ◆

*(Ed. Note: The following letter was received from the superintendent's office of District 99, Cicero (IL) Public Schools:*

*Thank you very much for coming to visit us. We know you have a busy schedule, but still you took time to come and visit us. We thoroughly enjoyed your visit and feel very honored and proud to have an 'Uncle George'. Thank you from the students of Rooms 212 and 301.*

◆    ◆    ◆

Is it fun to be a policeman? Do you have a gun? Did you ever fire it? How is it to be a policeman? Do you just go to schools when you want to, or dose someone send you there? It must be fun.—Fred

◆     ◆     ◆

One day I want to be a policeman like you. I would go to schools and visit the kids. I would help other people. I would catch a thief. I would keep on helping everyone.—Kevin

◆     ◆     ◆

I think you are the greatest and funniest policeman I ever met. Remember good-by in Italian is (ar-ree-vay-DAYR-chee).—Ellen

◆     ◆     ◆

Boy, I think you are a swell guy. I bet if you heard me say that, you would say "It makes me feel good all over."—Barbara

◆     ◆     ◆

When my brother was little, he drank something that was poison, and we had to give him vinegar. We put the poison symbol on it, and he never touched it again. Once I touched a stove, and I never touched one again. Just today, my friend was talking to a stranger, and I told him not to go by him because he might be bad. I'm lucky you reminded me. You know something. You make me feel good all over.—Scott

◆     ◆     ◆

Bring your wife sometime to school. Maybe I'll send some flowers.—Jeffrey

◆     ◆     ◆

I am doing my best in school. Jeff and Jessie are still bad, but the rest of us are good.—Love, Richard

◆     ◆     ◆

I hope you catch the robbers.—Mark

◆     ◆     ◆

I hope nobody escaped from you.—Christy

◆     ◆     ◆

I will not eat anything from strangers or very big strangers.—Your friend, UnSong

◆     ◆     ◆

You taught me a lot of things this year, last year, and the year before. I never listen to people when they call me into a car or give me candy or money, because I hate 'stranger-danger' and because they'll kill me. That's all I got to say.—Cindy

◆     ◆     ◆

I will not like Stranger-Danger cos they will try to kill me or might kidnap me. If an old lady or an old man told me to go in their house, 'I have some candy for you', would you go or take it? No. What will you say, 'mmmmm, I don't want any of that stouf', write? Yes.—Holly

◆     ◆     ◆

I want to know how you become a policeman. I think I want to be a policeman but I didn't make up my mind.—Keith

◆     ◆     ◆

One day, Stranger Danger wanted me to take a penny but I did not.—Carla

◆     ◆     ◆

I injoide your veseit, and I lrernd a loet, and I promes to stay out of my Mom and Dads medicine cabenit, and I promes to look four ways.—Love, Rhonda

◆     ◆     ◆

Room 114 will look four ways befor we gras the street. We all kiss the pictures of you Uncle George. And we hope your wife will have a baby too.—Diana

◆     ◆     ◆

I will be a policeman wen I gowrup.—Alex

◆     ◆     ◆

I will be a policeman when I am a man.—Love Kuo-Chan

◆     ◆     ◆

*(Ed. Note: The following excerpts show some serious thinking by a young girl):*

What do you think the Puerta Rican or Cuben people would do if they saw someone wearing their flag for socks? Our school children have seen a lot of things we don't like. We love our flag and salute it every morning. We love the boys who fight for U.S.A. but we do not like war. We pray war will stop. We are going to listen to you and our teacher, and do the good things you tell us to do because we can see that you are good people.—Kathy

◆　　◆　　◆

We are praying for some nice people to move in this neighborhood so we can live peacefully and have good friends. We had an answer to our prayer and got all the things we need to fix the windows (*in their church*) except someone to put them in.—Kathy

◆　　◆　　◆

I still have your picture in my desk. My teacher has your picture on the wall. We all remember your songs and we all love you very much. If it wasn't for you, we wouldn't know all about drugs.—Love, Pamela

◆　　◆　　◆

Thank you our wise Uncle George. I will thank you and I love you, I love you, I love you, and I love you. I will love you forever and ever.—Eric

◆　　◆　　◆

If someone gets a cold from another person, the other person goes to the doctor, the person who got the medicine should not give the other person his medicine. My dad used my red pills 5 times.—Philip

◆　　◆　　◆

I've listened to every word about medicine we are not supposed to take, and look two or four ways before we cross the street, and I learned about the traffic sign and about the traffic light.—John

◆　　◆　　◆

When I am big, I will still remember you and I will take your advice with me.—Love, Carla

◆     ◆     ◆

I still remember the day you visited our room when I was in third grade. You were so funny! I am going to remember you as long as I live.—Love, Donna

◆     ◆     ◆

I have your picture on my living room table. I look at it all the time.—Love, Cora

◆     ◆     ◆

I am very happy you came to my school. I know you did not have to come if you did not want to.—Love, your friend Fara

◆     ◆     ◆

I love you a hundred prousent.—You're my bet friend, Patricia

◆     ◆     ◆

I'm going to tell you about what running in the wrong crowd means to me. It means not to take medicine, drugs, not to sware, eat candy, or dope, do not drink. The End. I love you 100%.—Your friend, Karina

◆     ◆     ◆

The rong crowd means, like if somebody trys to give you some money, and you say 'I don't want any!' And he says, 'Why not', and I say 'because I don't like monies.' 'Then how about some candy?' 'No, I don't like that neither.' 'Why not?' 'That's because I'm not going to take anything you give me, so go away.'—I love you, Officer Friendly, better than candy and ice cream.—Your friend, Carl

◆   ◆   ◆

Thanky for taling us about drugs and thanky for taling us about sranjers.—Sergio

◆   ◆   ◆

Stranger-danger may seem nice, but if he can get you in his car, he will drive some place and do bad things to you. So I think when I grow up, I will be a police woman.—Caroline

◆   ◆   ◆

I think your very funny. I like you, and any time you want some freckles, just let me know.—Ingrid

◆   ◆   ◆

You are a smart man. You are the nicest person I ever saw. I love you very, very much, and I always will as long as I live.—Lori

◆   ◆   ◆

You teached me a lot. I have been bad some times, but nobody's perfect, so I am behaving now, and I am old enough to take care of myself.—Bobby

◆   ◆   ◆

I hope you will forgive the messingness and unneatness.—Linda S.

◆   ◆   ◆

I got a pretty good report card but I have a F in Math. My mother said if I don't get a good mark on my report card, I will get in trouble again.—John

◆     ◆     ◆

My sister is still drinking and sometimes get in fights. I hope you can still help her. If you can, I will be glad. I think you are the best cop. I do.—Michelle

◆     ◆     ◆

I agree with you, drugs are N.G. That means No Good. I always practice my safety rules.—Michael

◆     ◆     ◆

You are a nice officer. I am doing find and I am not take dope because you said so.—Love, Adam

◆     ◆     ◆

I like you very much. So does my sister. I wish you would come to Prescott School every week. I only take medicine when my Mother tells me to. I like the idea of you teaching children about drugs. My little brother is coming to Prescott School soon. He will like you too.—Your friend, Tammy

◆     ◆     ◆

Thank you for teaching me all that you did. I think you've been very nice since I've known you, that is from kindergarten through 4th grade. I know what I will miss you. I hope to see you again some day because I think you're nice. I will not take drugs without my parents permission. Thank you.—Elizabeth

◆     ◆     ◆

I'm a loyal fan of yours. Thank you for the pictures. We're going to hang them up in our room when its remodeled.—Your fan, Billy

◆     ◆     ◆

I think we have the best country in the world. My friends who come from other countries tell me how lucky I am to have a free and beautiful country. I know that is true. I also know, bad people who are jelus of my country and want to hurt it.—Nancy

◆     ◆     ◆

Thank you for the candies and Halloween bags. This letter is what you deserve from me for a thank you. I missed you all summer. I didn't have something to do but play. I hated to play so I thought about what you told about DRUGS and so I thought about someone taking DRUGS. I kept on thinking if one of my brothers or sister took the wrong pill, neither one will die or get sick. I know what this sign *(poison logo)* means to me. It means drugs and to keep out of reach of children.—Eulogio T., Jr.

◆     ◆     ◆

We've been having some trouble with the gangs. I wish we could get rid of them. I wish they would get saved and come to Christ. We're always praying for you.—Lucy

◆     ◆     ◆

I am making something for you. I hope you like it. It won't be too good. If you want to, you can throw it away.—Karen

◆     ◆     ◆

Some of my friends say the police are no good, they just get everyone in trouble, but I don't think so and I tell them so.—Lisa

◆     ◆     ◆

Thank you for being so nice and treating us to lunch.—Marie

◆　　◆　　◆

Thank you for coming to our school and telling us about your interesting job. It was a truly interesting discussion. We think that the Officer Friendly program is a good idea. You must work very hard at your job in helping people. We learned things we never knew.—Cindy

◆　　◆　　◆

You are funny. I like it when you shake your hips.—Vicky

◆　　◆　　◆

When I grow up I want to be nice and happy like you.—Italina

◆　　◆　　◆

I will like to ask you what I should do with a purse that I found on the sidewalk near my house. There was no name on any of the papers ion it. There was some paper money and some small coins in it. Here is my phone number so you can tell me what should I do.—Maria

◆　　◆　　◆

When you visited my class you said, "This is the last time I can come to your room." I really hate to see you go. I really, really love you, so much that I really hate for you to go.—Mary

◆　　◆　　◆

I now you love me and you now that I love you too. So I wish you were my boyfriend. Don't think it's a lie cause it's not. I love you so much that I can kiss you the next time I see you.—Donna

◆     ◆     ◆

I hope you are having lots of fun being a policeman and going to all the schools in Chicago.—Kimberly

◆     ◆     ◆

I love you like one of the family.—Maria

◆     ◆     ◆

I would want to be your son but I can't. I have to stay put. Some day I am not going to be a policeman. I am going to be a fireman. I want to put out fires and save peoples lives. I like the training they do.—John

◆     ◆     ◆

You said that next year in 5th grade we will not have you any more. I sure hope I didn't hear you right. One of my real uncles is a policeman, and I don't care what other people say. I love policemen dearly.—Phyllis

◆     ◆     ◆

My Mom said that the picture you gave me was the prettiest picture she ever saw.—Danette

◆     ◆     ◆

You should go on a diet and not eat to much.—Maria

◆     ◆     ◆

I am Polish and Spanish, mostly Spanish, and don't forget to put your gun in your pocket instead of your toothbrush.—Jackie

◆     ◆     ◆

Since you're my best friend, I wish you were my father because maybe my mother would never get divorced. My father sometimes asks my mother for twenty-five dollars.—David

◆     ◆     ◆

Gus what, we got a new pope *(puppy)* and its name is Mikea, and it is quaet.—Connie.

◆     ◆     ◆

When you left Room 207, I swall to God that I crided for you. When I stopped crying, I said a pier for you. I wanted to tell you that I am an acto-light. An actolight is a boy that is 11 years old and lights the candels on the allto. God bless you Uncle George, and I swall to God I love you. Good-by. God bless you and good luck.—Ronald

◆     ◆     ◆

I think you make a lot of sense. I've been offered cigarettes seven times. Once I refused a couple of kids, and they punch me around, but I'm glad I refused. I'll never accept cigarettes or smoke them. I promise!!! (unsigned)

◆     ◆     ◆

I like you, you are funny! I am a girl but I will like to know what kind of shooter you have. For example, like a 28 shooter. I wish you really was my uncle. My Mother works at Victors office machines. My Father works in a store on Belmont on the first floor in men's underwear.—Yvette

*(Ed. Note: that last line above "works in men's underwear", hmmm, reminiscent of an old vaudeville gag.)*

◆　　　◆　　　◆

I am so glad you came to our prayer meeting downstairs with us. Do you remember we prayed for our church to be painted, and the Lord answered our prayer. We found some men who painted our church. I hope some day you can come and see it.—Jelena

◆　　　◆　　　◆

Are you only an Officer Friendly, or are you a policeman too?—Maria

◆　　　◆　　　◆

My hole class loves you, but I love you more than I love anybody in the world.—Lori

I wish my father was a polisman. I like when you twist your but. When I grow up, I am going to be a nurse cause I know a lot now about medicines, drugs and poison.—Vicky

◆　　　◆　　　◆

You are right about crime going up. The other day my aunt was in school when a bunch of girls came up to her and asked her for money. When she refused, they tried to take it away from her. When she tried to fight them off, one pulled a knife and put several deep wounds in her arm. When this was over, they ran but without the money. This has happened to my brother several times. In our neighborhood there are very many gangs. When they are not fighting with their fists or bottles or bats, they're fighting with guns or trying to run each other down with cars. A month ago, a man got his head split wide open WITH HIS BRAINS HANGING OUT.—George

◆　　　◆　　　◆

Some people last night were driving motorcycles really fast and came back and forth on a one-way street.—Paulina

◆　　　◆　　　◆

I am writing fast because I am in a hurry. This is a very, very, very, very, very, very, very short letter. I wrote VERY 7 times because it will make the letter longer.—Pamela

◆     ◆     ◆

I hope you will have no trouble on your police force. How many are there in the whole station? I hope you are safe when your on duty. One day my brother was sitting in his room on the first floor. Someone threw a rock through the window and shattered the glass and cut my brother.—Fred

◆     ◆     ◆

How is it being an Officer? Well I think it's a very nice job, and I'm sure you do too. I think an Officer is very good even though my father isn't one, and I'm a girl. What does an Officer do? Do they have fun? How many Officers are in the police department?—Jenny

◆     ◆     ◆

I love Jesus. I hope you love him too. I hope that you hate the Devil.—Holly

◆     ◆     ◆

How many men are there in your force? I like fishing, camping, car racing, baseball, football, swimming, hockey, track and field. I hope you catch all the robbers.—Fred

◆     ◆     ◆

What do you do if you are caught and kidnapped? What do you do if you are lost and you can't find a policeman?—Debra

◆     ◆     ◆

Our crossing guard said you are the best friend we could have. You will always help if we need you.—Dragana

◆     ◆     ◆

This letter will make you feel good all over. You are one of the best police I know. We have hamsters and their names are Jack and Jill. And we have a dog to and its name is Satan. We had a cat but it died. But we all cryed because the cat died so my Dad bought us another cat and we named it Pinky.—Steven

◆     ◆     ◆

I wish you would write a letter back. If you do I will like you more than ever. OK? Bye.—Christine

◆     ◆     ◆

How do you feel? Did you chase anyone bad?—Evelyn

◆     ◆     ◆

I hate you. I don't like you. I LOVE you.—Dawn

◆     ◆     ◆

I'm sorry that I took up to much time, but an 8 year old got a lot to say in a letter to his favorite policeman hero. Good-bye and Good Luck.—Your Admirer, Eugene

◆     ◆     ◆

Thank you for the book and card and visudeenus.—Christine

◆     ◆     ◆

I make this letter short because I know you have other more important things to do, Uncle George!—Your friend, Michelle

◆        ◆        ◆

I promise to take no candy from nobuty.—Your friend, Donna

◆        ◆        ◆

I think you are the best officer in the worl. I wont take nothink that the peo-ple give to me becus it cood have drugs. I will tall mi father to not smoke.—Jannette

◆        ◆        ◆

I'll hang your picture up and never take it down—Anita

◆        ◆        ◆

I saw the skellation *(skeleton)* on Drano. I piked it up and I saw it and I droped it and ran in my room.—Love, Donna (P.S. I'm the girl that was in the red shirt, blue pants, and white vest.)

◆        ◆        ◆

I'm not one for writeing a letter. I am writeing fast because I am in a hurry.—Love, Pamela

◆        ◆        ◆

One of the children in our room is going to make an eagle with the tops of cans.—Your friend, Pauline

◆        ◆        ◆

I like all the things you tout us. The teacher is pudding a sine on the board so if we talk, we have to put a check by are name. I love you uncle G.P. stands for Georgie Porgie. We all love you and your son and your wilf. I hop you can bring more pichers of your son, and pleay's rite back to me.—Goodby, Monica

♦     ♦     ♦

I love you more than I love anybody in the world. I wanted to ask you if you still had your Mickey Mouse t-shirt on. But I don't care about Mickey Mouse as long as I got you for a friend. I don't think I whould want anybody better. I love you and Mickey Mouse.—Lori

♦     ♦     ♦

I remember when you taught me about the skull, that it means don't go near it. I obey you because if you didn't tell me, I can be dead right now. What can I do then?—Kim

♦     ♦     ♦

I only went Trick or Treat on my block. I only got about 20 or 25 pieces of candy. My brothers and sisters ate most of my Trick and Treat candy. Will you wright back? But if you don't have a knuf time to, that is OK. I half to go know, by.—Love, Corin

♦     ♦     ♦

How many years have you been Officer Friendly? Please pray that no one will be able to break the new windows we have put in the Church.—Your friend, Mona

♦     ♦     ♦

I always say hellow to police man that I see, enless there in a car. I watch out for stoplights and stopsigns. I stay away from turning cars and buses. I watch out for stranger danger too. Once there was a stranger and my sister said that he broke into a car and two dogs bit his hand off. My sister new them and there masters.—Your friend, Tracy

◆         ◆         ◆

We could be pen pals. Don't laugh because it's true. I'd really like it if you could, but if you can't it's OK too.—Love, your friend (I hope), Rose

◆         ◆         ◆

I have been waiting to write to you but I didn't get around to it. Yesterday I was planning to but I couldn't find your address. My mother found it so than I started. I saw you in the newspaper, that's when I remembered.—Michelle

◆         ◆         ◆

Please write back if you have the time to I mean. If you want we can become pen pals. If you want, and only when you have the time. Please write back soon. Bye!!—Love, Sincerely, Your honest friend, Your's truly, Rose

◆         ◆         ◆

I'll try to do my best for you. I hope you do not kill anyone cause that is sad for you. I hope you do not get hurt.—Love, Zolena

◆         ◆         ◆

I am sending you two box tops of Carnation Instant breakfast and Raisin Bran cereal to show you what I'm eating.—Yours truly, Sandra

◆         ◆         ◆

I think we should have more policemen like you because you love chedln vear much.—Martin

◆     ◆     ◆

You are my very best friend. All policemen are my friends. Tell them that.—Your Bunny, Louise

◆     ◆     ◆

*(Ed. Note: Another testimonial from a grade school teacher):*

> *Thank you for coming to our school last week. Your presentation not only delightful but also informative. Both the children and I enjoyed your visit. We hope you will come to see us again soon and are looking forward to receiving your pictures.—Rochelle*

◆     ◆     ◆

I hope you had a good time with us because I had a good time with you. Oh, you were so Marvoules!—Love, Catherine

◆     ◆     ◆

When you were going to leave, I was going to cry because I love you so much that I wish you would live with me.—Estella

◆     ◆     ◆

*(Ed. Note: This is a THIRD letter from 'Rose' now in a higher grade.)*

You were my Officer Friendly in 5th grade, I think, or was it 4th? I'm still in the same nice school, but I'm in the 7th grade now. PLEASE, if you have ANY time, PLEASE write back to me.—Rose

◆     ◆     ◆

Chicago Police Department, you help me a lot by looking for ways.—Nina

◆     ◆     ◆

I am the one who had wrote to you and you answered it but I never wrote back. I am very sorry for not writing cause I was in the hospital so many times that I could not write you back.—Debbie

◆     ◆     ◆

I am your peter rabbit. The whole class misses you.—your Peter Rabbit, Frank

◆     ◆     ◆

I heard a lot about dope and robbing on the news.—Stacy

◆     ◆     ◆

I remember what you told us about medicines, poison and wicked men.—Your friend, Kathy

◆     ◆     ◆

My brother got maryed Saturday, and I cried because I did not want to see him go.—Love, Don

◆     ◆     ◆

Could you come over to my hose and stay for about 10 or 20 mines? Well I got to go. I will see you when you come at school or at my hose.—Love, Connie

◆　　◆　　◆

When I grow up I might even be a policeman like you!—Yours truly, Juan (*P.S. Now I have to Uncles!*)

◆　　◆　　◆

How is baby Friendly? I hope he is fine. I had a good Hallowean. I did wut you told us to do.—Your friend, Troy

◆　　◆　　◆

(*Ed. Note: The following letter was completely covered in hand-drawn hearts but contained only ONE sentence*):

I love you and my parents.—Cathy

◆　　◆　　◆

I wish you could have dinner with me but I know you have a buzy segual.—Linda

◆　　◆　　◆

You are a good person that takes care of all the children, and you are a very very special person.—from your friends Gina and Carol

◆　　◆　　◆

(*Ed. note: The following letter also contained only ONE sentence but was very simply stated in printed words TWO INCHES TALL*):

YOU ARE A GOOD POLICE MAN.—Brett

◆       ◆       ◆

I will never rob anybody because I will go to jail. Please teach us more about police because when I grow up I am going to be a police man.—Love, Ruben

◆       ◆       ◆

I would like another picture of you because my dog got my other one.—Sincerely, Christine

◆       ◆       ◆

I like to listen about playing with maches, and don't take diop, and don't smoke and some other thinks.—Your friend, Jane

◆       ◆       ◆

I swear to never take drugs or pills and dope, and when someone comes up and say, 'I've got some old bikes, do you want one?', I would say 'no'.—Love, Joseph

◆       ◆       ◆

Can I have two pictures of you and make two fake badges for us and some police cards and some WANTED posters.—Cathy

◆       ◆       ◆

I watched a movie called "Go Ask Alice". It was about a girl who was on drugs. I wish you could come and talk to us more about drug abuse.—Sincerely, Jessica

◆   ◆   ◆

I like it very much when you come to visit us because you always teach us a good lesson about teenagers and drugs today, and it is wonderful to have an Officer like you to teach us that stuff. I wish that I knew how a police station looks and what kind of work you do there too.—Laura

◆   ◆   ◆

Thank you for the burgher king doll. I wish that you could come more often. We really like you. You were right. You cant trust people these days.—Yours truly, Nidia

◆   ◆   ◆

One day when my cousin David and my friend Gary and I were playing in the alley, we saw a police car. He drove down the alley and asked us why we were not in school. We said 'We were off for Easter vacation'. Uncle George, this story is true.—Your friend, the red head, Scott

◆   ◆   ◆

If you ever have any more educational movies, we'll be glad to see them.—Your friend, Lucy

◆   ◆   ◆

*(Ed. Note: A Student Teacher sadly reflected):*

> *Many times the image of a public servant is ignorantly portrayed, for instance, the police as a pig-like figure and a teacher like a dictator of an imprisoned concentration camp. YOU have combined what I feel is so badly lacking, and have shown that there are still 'Uncle Georges' in the world. DON'T STOP!*

◆     ◆     ◆

Yesterday there was a fire but I did not see it but they told me. That same night there was a bad accident near our house. A motorcycle was speeding on the yellow line in the middle of the street and crashed into a car. The man on the motorcycle must have been drunk. There was a gang on the corner. The man in the car took off. He was probably afraid of the gang he saw on the corner.—Yours truly, Nancy

◆     ◆     ◆

You are the second one I like. The first one is my daddy. I love him and you the best. I get Officer Friendly books from my daddy and YOU! My father is a Officer Friendly from the 13th District.—As ever, Marcello

◆     ◆     ◆

*(Ed. Note: The following is typical of the testimonials from parents):*

> *Thank you for teaching my daughter and the children at her school. As a working mother, I appreciate the time and effort, and most of all your concern.—Mrs. Lucille G.*

◆     ◆     ◆

I will stay away from poison, and I will teach my sister about poison and say what you said so she nows about poison so she would stay out of the medison and wont get sick, case I love her and I love my mom and dad and you.—Rebecca

◆     ◆     ◆

Are you working hard and earning lots of money? I hope that you and your wife and children make out good.—Jorene

◆    ◆    ◆

I remember the story you told about Johnny whose mother never told him not to steal. When he was 5 years old, he started stealing little things like candy, and when he became 6 years old he stole a bike. His mom said 'good boy, John'. When he was 16, he stole a car and said, 'Look, Mom, I stole a car', and she said, 'Good bye, John'.—Jane

◆    ◆    ◆

If somebody says 'do you want some of this?' You say, 'chhhhh, I don't want any of that stuff'.—Ursula

◆    ◆    ◆

*(Ed. Note: A third-grade teacher wrote as follows):*

*Our 3 $^{rd}$ -graders had already written you these invitations to attend our Valentine's Day party before they discovered you would be busy that day. I promised them I would mail these letters anyway.—From your growing 'fan club'.*

◆    ◆    ◆

This is only a little letter because I didn't know what to write.—Catherine

◆    ◆    ◆

I didn't make so good on my report card. All I made was 1 G, 2 F, 1B, 2 E. The other day my friend almost got run over. He was riding a bike across the street. I always push my bike across the street.—Tony

◆     ◆     ◆

I made a Hawaiian Lay and gave it to you when you visited our class room. Would you please send me a picture of you?—Paula

◆     ◆     ◆

If I was a teenager and saw a person selling dope, I will call the police and I hope they will arrest him.—Paul David

◆     ◆     ◆

We read something from the crime books this morning. Say hello to your family for me.—Harold

◆     ◆     ◆

I love you very much. I hope you like my father who works for the Salvation Army.—Alan

◆     ◆     ◆

You are much pretty then the other Officer Friendly.  Here's a picture of you.
You'r holding the kids back, the cars and trucks pass buy. - Sonia

# JOHN PATRICK FAHEY

*("Father" Fahey)*

Commander, 19<sup>th</sup> Police District 1959–1970

A change of heart toward becoming a priest resulted in his joining the Chicago Police Department in 1932 for a career that spanned 38 years to retirement.

His mother may have been disappointed that he had chosen a different vocation, but, if she had lived to see the man he became, and the good that he had done, she would surely have approved his decision. His image and philosophy emulated that of a relationship between a shepherd and his flock.

He was promoted to Sergeant in 1947 after serving with the Army in Panama during World War II. He was promoted to Lieutenant in 1954, and made Captain in 1959 when he was assigned to the 19<sup>th</sup> (Town Hall) Police District as Commander.

During his tenure at Town Hall, he conducted classes in the public schools on police work and became actively effective in the community through innovative programs he established: "Bringing Up Father", stressing the importance of leading, not driving, their teens; and the "Junior Patrol" program for elementary school children (later adopted city-wide) to encourage youth to learn about and respect law enforcement. He said of his work with young people, "If I've kept one boy from stealing a car or one girl from shoplifting, the whole program has been worthwhile."

His advice to the men, who came to him with marital problems, began with the suggestion that they should always refer to one's wife as 'my bride'. It bodes better than referring to her disrespectfully as 'my old lady' which is negative and demeaning. Speaking to young people in language they could understand, he advised, "When another boy or girl dares you to commit a crime lest you be called "chicken", tell that boy or girl that you'll still be a 'free' chicken when they are in the 'chicken coop' to stay!"

In 1962, the Lake View Citizens Council named him "Policeman of the Year"; and, in 1969, he received the Lake View community's annual "Brotherhood Award."

The Lake View community turned out en masse for a testimonial assembly at Lane Technical High School for his retirement. He passed away in April of 1986.

# SUFFER LITTLE CHILDREN
# TO COME UNTO ME

The one common denominator shared world-wide by law enforcement officers is their compassion for children. The title quotation above comes from the Bible (Mark:10:14) and came to mind because of the image I saw every time I passed by Commander Fahey's office: there would always be children crowded around him, sitting on his desk, standing beside or behind him, all speaking at once. He patiently answered their questions, listened to their stories, and told some of his own. It validated why he wore the affectionate title of "Father" Fahey.

The police station was 'kid friendly'. There was always a steady stream of boys who came in to pick up a Junior Patrol membership application. He would tell them to take it home and go over it with their parents, fill it out, and then return it to the office girl FRIDAY. That's how my colleague and good friend, Regina, got the nickname "Friday". The boys assumed her name was "Friday", and that monicker stuck.

Commander Fahey stressed the importance to the Junior Patrol boys, the importance of respecting the ownership of one's name—the one thing that exclusively belongs to each of us. "Reggie", as I called her, and I managed to shoot down that premise one day. At best, we were guilty of a faux pas, to wit:

A boy came in one time who was hesitant to give his name. She and I tried to explain that everyone should be proud of his name. We informed him that we needed it so we could mail a notice to him and his parents of when and where the next swearing-in ceremony would take place. Finally, after gentle goading, he weakened and spelled his last name for us:

C-A-C-C-I-A-T-O-R-E. She and I blurted out simultaneously, "Does anyone ever call you 'chicken'?" He gave us a 'look', turned on his heel, and left—not acknowledging our awkward apologies, and was probably scarred for life.

In another brilliant instance, as a boy came in and requested a Junior Patrol questionnaire, Regina handed it to him, and said, "THERE YOU GO". Taking it literally, he took it, looked around, and asked "WHERE?" He didn't understand that it was a figure of speech. We really weren't trying to be rude, but, whenever Regina saw him approaching after that (and he did make frequent visits), she'd give me a warning whisper, *"Here comes WHERE!"*

# JUNIOR POLICE PATROL

### *Membership Questionnaire*

With the help of your family, study these facts, check each one, and decide whether it is *TRUE* or *FALSE*. If it is *TRUE*, mark "T" after the statement. If it is *FALSE*, mark "F" after the statement. When completed, return it to the District Commander or Officer Friendly.

1) Every member of the Junior Patrol is an important person. _____

2) Every person has a mission in life. _____

3) People are born to succeed, not to fail. _____

4) Learn to get along with people. _____

5) Learn to put yourself in the other person's place. _____

6) If you are angry, think before you speak, or ACT. _____

7) A good citizen observes the law. _____

8) A person is known by his conduct. _____

9) If you don't smoke cigarettes, don't start. _____

10) One example is worth a thousand arguments. _____

11) Responsibility is taught by example. _____

12) Don't make excuses—make GOOD. _____

13) No one is a failure until he gives up. _____

14) Treat everyone with politeness, even those who are rude to you. _____

15) By following the good, you learn to be good. _____

16) The person who gossips TO you, will gossip ABOUT you. _____

17) Honesty is the first chapter in the book of Wisdom. _____

18) Ignorance costs more than education in the long run. _____

19) Truancy is the first symptom of delinquency.                                   ____

20) Truth is the foundation of all knowledge.                                      ____

21) A boy or girl is never well-dressed until they wear a smile.                    ____

22) It is much easier to KEEP OUT of trouble than to GET OUT of trouble.           ____

23) Know the value of time, and use every moment of it.                            ____

24) Forgiveness is better than revenge.                                            ____

25) Forgiveness is the sign of a noble nature and a real gentleman.                ____

26) Crime is reduced by common sense.                                              ____

27) The success or failure of a person depends on his willpower.                   ____

28) If a person makes a mistake, he should try to correct it.                      ____


_____

**Signature of Parent or Guardian**

*If the answer to all or most of these questions is TRUE, then the Junior Police Patrol applicant is on the right track. If any of the answers is FALSE, investigate and help to place him on the right track.*

# "FATHER" FAHEY'S RETIREMENT"

The boys a cappella choir and I conspired to do something original and special to bid adieu to the much-loved Commander. First on the list was an idea that we would propose to the District's friends at WGN-TV: to arrange for air transportation for Commander Fahey's daughter, Mary, a student in Mexico, to arrive secretly and surprise him on the event stage. Good! They agreed to finance the trip and sequester her until her surprise entrance on the stage at the testimonial.

Meanwhile, 'back at the ranch', I got busy fashioning a bull costume from a lamp shade head and a burlap body. I rehearsed two boys to wear it and make some comical movements, while the rest of the choir would sing "Ferdinand, the Bull". That would be a clue for Mary to come out on stage, all the way from Mexico! It worked perfectly. Commander Fahey said he had never received such a wonderful present—his daughter, not the bull! Mrs. Fahey, and Mary's siblings, Nancy and Patrick, were equally ecstatic.

Commander Fahey was a brilliant, honest and humble man, devoid of any prejudice or pretentiousness. He went 'by the book'. He didn't 'fix' things like traffic citations. He always answered related requests that it would have to be 'adjudicated in court'.

He was soft-spoken but firm, with a convincing countenance and persuasive manner, and a good sense of humor. One day, he recounted the various situations where he was fortunate to talk an offender into submission. One of those incidents involved a police woman who requested back-up. She was being threatened by a man wielding a wicked-looking large knife. When Commander arrived at the scene, he calmly suggested to the aggressor, "Why don't you give me the knife before somebody gets hurt?" The man quickly acquiesced without hesitation.

Police officers have to make scheduled appearances at the range with their regulation weapons, and their scores become part of their permanent record. The Commander stood in the center of our clerical office one day, took his gun from his holster, looked at it and said it was about time for him to go down to the range, but he wondered if it would work or if it might have rusted tight—then admitting he had never fired a gun in his entire law enforcement career. Incredible, I thought!

He was a role model for the men under his command, with an open-door policy to listen to them, their spouses, any child or citizen who came to him with questions or complaints. His posture was that of a benevolent cleric, reflecting the years he spent in a seminary where, just prior to taking his final vows toward priesthood, he decided he might be better suited to be a husband and father. It was obvious he had made the right choice. He often quipped, "It was a good day when my mother and father caught the boat (from Ireland) to come to this country."

# Chicago Police Department

## 𝕳onor Award

THIS IS TO CERTIFY THAT

_merits commendation for participation in the_

19th District
BOYS CHOIR

_Francis P. Nolan_      _James B. Conlisk Jr._

FRANCIS P. NOLAN             JAMES B. CONLISK, JR.
19th District Commander         Superintendent of Police

_Dated this_____ _day of_____

# $19^{th}$ DISTRICT JUNIOR PATROL BOYS A CAPPELLA CHOIR

Another program connecting youth with police personnel was on the horizon. This would involve music—open to boys, ages 6 to 16, who were not interested or not physically able to participate in the ongoing sports programs, as well as those who were already involved in the baseball and football activities.

This would be a 'first' for the police department. With my background of music education and performance experience in community theatre, I had the credentials and desire to direct a boys' a cappella choir. It would be a year 'round activity, not seasonal like the sports programs. It would not require the purchase of equipment nor the ability to read music as it would be taught by rote.

My proposal was enthusiastically received by the District Commander and downtown headquarters personnel. I was ready. I had already prepared material: vocal arrangements based on familiar tunes that were suitable for young boys' changing voices. I received professional support from Rosario Lombardo, director of my parish choir and supervisor of choral music for Chicago public schools.

The repertoire included traditional compositions with a kid-friendly twist as well as parodies that held a serious message subliminally wrapped in humor. Using the roster of Junior Patrol boys helped to form the nucleus of the choir. Their enthusiasm was encouraging enough for me to canvass schools and churches in the area. Soon there was a membership of nearly 90 boys. Most of them could carry a tune. They drowned out the ones that couldn't.

Of course, no one was refused membership, not even the six-year-old twins who always sang a little flat. I suggested they 'think' higher, which usually helps. They had a better solution: they stood on tiptoes!

A central location for rehearsals was offered at my parish with the blessing of the pastor, Monsignor Quinn, in spite of the fact that the parish Bingo operation had recently been shut down in accordance with legislation. We were given the use of a basement classroom to rehearse after school hours, complete with the luxury of an on-site piano.

The boys came from all corners of the District: the German-Irish population on the west side, to the newly-arrived Hispanic contingency in the center, and the affluent Gold Coast residents of the east end on Lake Shore Drive.

The boys were amazing. They learned the songs quickly and were eager to perform. As we were invited to perform at various venues, I added skits appropriate for the various audiences which I composed, choreographed, and costumed. They added humor while delivering serious messages: about con games to dupe senior citizens; become a victim of Stranger Danger; the need to report suspicious activities, the rewards of being a good neighbor; and that police officers are their friends.

Superintendent Conlisk obviously was impressed by authorizing every member to receive a blue long-sleeved dress shirt, black tie, and a personalized gold name plate engraved with his name—emulating the uniform worn by Chicago patrolmen. The parents were as proud and grateful as the boys.

Weekly rehearsals were conducted from 4:00-5:00 P.M., giving the children enough time to get there after school and to get home in time for dinner. Every week, I had free meal coupons generously donated by MacDonald's to treat six to eight boys as I drove them home in my choir-size old Pontiac station wagon. That was such an impressive treat for them—especially for the ones who were used to beans and rice every day instead of meat and potatoes.

Occasionally, I received permission from some parents to let their son be my houseguest for a day. It was a good way to introduce ethnicities to my children who were excited to host a special guest and willing to give up their room for the overnight. I had an old three-story Victorian house which was simply furnished with hand-me-down furniture that fascinated the visitors who came from large families that lived in crowded, smaller places.

It always amazed me that those boys who joined the choir really wanted to sing, rather than swing (a baseball bat), considering the home environment in which many of them lived—some with gang connections in their own families. The excuses for absences from rehearsals were not the usual 'Johnny was sick' ones. One boy confided, "I had to miss rehearsal because I had to go to court because my father raped my sister". Another one said, "I had to babysit my little brother and sister because my mother and father were arrested for running a bunko (gambling) game"(a common activity at the time).

Although I conducted rehearsals and performances by myself, it was a credit to these boys that I had no discipline problems. They responded to the fact that I was honest with them, not condescending, and really cared about them—and I really did. I tried to be fair in my expectations of their behavior as well as their talent, always striving to make it a fun but still a learning experience.

Deputy Chief Lynsky confirmed that fact when he introduced our group at Headquarters for a Christmas performance, "The really good show is at their rehearsals." He had dropped in unannounced at the rehearsal when I was teaching a soft-shoe routine for two boys to the tune "Cecilia". Later, at the retirement party for Commander Fahey, I had two boys in a bull costume I crafted for the inimitable hysterical moves as the rest of the choir sang "Ferdinand, the Bull". It introduced the surprise appearance of his daughter, Mary, who was studying in Mexico but brought to the retirement via courtesy of WGN-TV.

The choir performed at a variety of venues: a high-rise for seniors; a retired nuns' residence; a downtown alcoholics treatment center; a live broadcast on WGN-TV; at a Christmas Eve Midnight Mass at St. Andrew Church; some ice cream socials; at Police Headquarters at Christmas; and at Soldier Field for the Police-Fire Thrill Show. I know what it feels like to walk the length of Soldier Field because, as we were about to perform, our fifteen minutes of fame was cut to five minutes by some programming interloper.

I marched to the other end of the field where Superintendent Conlisk had policemen lined up at attention, waiting to make their entrance. I went up to the Superintendent to tell him his orders for our 15-minute segment had been pre-empted by this disturbing gentleman. We had worked so hard to polish our presentation which included the anthem I had composed for the City of Chicago. He radioed the emcee to allow us to proceed with our program as planned.

As to that anthem, when I told the boys I wrote it about Chicago's motto and asked if anyone knew the motto's two words. Hands shot up, "I know, I know", said one boy, "It's WHERE'S MINE?"

For all of our performances, the Police Department sent two buses to pick up the boys and any of their friends and relatives who wanted to join us. That was just another example of the support of any programs for youth.

We started every public performance with the boys entering the room, moving through the audience, singing, "Hi, Neighbor", while shaking hands in the crowd until they got to the stage area. Then, in unison, they introduced me a la Johnny Carson show opening, "And now, he-e-e-e-r-e's Joanie."

# INITIAL ROSTER OF JUNIOR PATROL A CAPPELLA CHOIR MEMBERS

R. Badillo

P. Buchanan

D. Dienethal

B. Fagan

P. Foley

J. Holmberg

J. Irwin

J. Jacks

J. Lopez

T. Mahn

A. Ortega

J. Perez

J. Reed, Jr.

M. Ruffner

M. Sabaduquia

J. Scanlan

K. Shuttleworth

J. Smerda

J. Umana

E. Ziemba

R. Bauknecht

M. Campos

E. Dienethal, Jr.

D. Featherston

A. Goosinow

J. Hopkins

B. Jacobson

B. Lidman

J. Mahn

S. Mason

J. Paschke

W. Perez

S. Richmond

S. Ruffner

E. Santiago

J. Schulz

K. Shuttleworth

A. Spalding

M. Walz

B. Zimmer

M. Buchanan

P. Carrera

R. Dienethal

R. Feliciano

C. Goosinow

E. Howard

J. Jacobson

D. Lidman

S. Mahn

L. Mion

A. Perez

J. Reed

D. Rosario

N. Sabaduquia

`J. Santiago

P. Schulz

R. Shuttleworth

H. Spalding

R. Warda

R. Ziebell

# *REPERTOIRE*

*19<sup>th</sup> District Junior Patrol*
*A Cappella Choir*

## *(Alphabetically)*

1. **Ballin' the Jack (dance duo)**
2. **Cecilia (soft-shoe routine)**
3. **Dear 019 (parody of 'Sweet Adeline')**
4. **Fahey (Mary), It's a Grand Old Name**
5. **Ferdinand, the Bull (in costume)**
6. **Give a Little Whistle**
7. **Hi, Neighbor (performance opener)**
8. **I Believe (vocal solo)**
9. **Keep the Spirit (to the tune of:Battle Hymn of the Republic)**
10. **Let a Winner Lead the Way**
11. **M-O-T-H-E-R**
12. **Old McDonald Had a Farm (parody)**
13. **Our Boys Will Shine Tonight**
14. **P-O-5 1-3-1-3**
15. **Sonny Boy (vaudeville duet)**
16. **Stranger-Danger (skits)(Satan Takes a Holiday)**
17. **Walking Happy**
18. **Whistle a Happy Tune**

## HI, NEIGHBOR!

(sung to the audience, by the boys
as they entered performance venue,
and shook hands with everyone)

Hi, Neighbor—Hi, Neighbor
What d'ya know,
And what d'ya say?

Hi, Neighbor—Hi, Neighbor,
Throw all your troubles away.

Come on and shake my hand,
And let a grin do the rest.
It makes ya' feel so grand,
To get your chin off your chest.

We're shouting, "Hi, Neighbor, Hi, Neighbor",
Time to play and say "Hi".

◆　　　◆　　　◆

## DEAR 019 (tune: 'Sweet Adeline')

Dear 019, Our 019

We sing of you, the Men in Blue
        Of 019, Our 019.

On our hearts, we wear a star,
        For 019, dear 019.

◆　　　◆　　　◆

## OUR BOYS WILL SHINE TONIGHT

Our boys will shine tonight, our boys will shine.
Our boys will shine tonight, all down the line.

Our boys will shine tonight, our boys will shine.
When the sun goes down, and the moon comes up,
OUR BOYS WILL SHINE.

The following parody was based on the emergency police number:

P O 5—1 3 1 3

before the number "9 1 1" was universally adopted:

## JUNIOR PATROL "FIGHT" SONG

(A parody on "Doe, A Deer" from "Sound of Music)

P O 5—1 3 1 3 CALL WHEN YOU SEE SOMETHING WRONG
P O 5—1 3 1 3 HELP IS WAITING ALL DAY LONG.

YOU MAY HELP TO CATCH A THIEF,
SAVE SOMEONE FROM LOTS OF GRIEF,
WHEN YOU CALL YOUR FRIENDS IN BLUE.
HELP IS WAITING THERE FOR YOU-OO-OO-OO,

P O 5—1 3 1 3 LEARN TO USE YOUR EYES AND EARS.
P O 5—1 3 1 3 THAT'S THE NUMBER BAD GUYS FEAR.

YOU DON'T HAVE TO GIVE YOUR NAME.
HELP IS WAITING JUST THE SAME.
WHEN THE JOB CALLS FOR A COP,
CALL 'OPERATION CRIME STOP'.

P O 5—1 3 1 3

## Variations on 'OLD McDONALD'S FARM

| | |
|---|---|
| Old McDonald had a farm | E I E I O |
| And on his farm he had some chicks | E I E I O |

With a chick, chick, here

And a chick, chick, there

Here a chick, there a chick

Chickens in every coop.

If those chickens get out of line—

CHICKEN NOODLE SOUP!

| | |
|---|---|
| Old McDonald had a farm, | E I E I O |
| And on his farm he had some cows, | E I E I O |

With a moo moo here,

And a moo moo there,

Here a moo, there a moo.

Cows just everywhere.

If those cows get out of line:

HAMBURGER, MEDIUM RARE!

| | |
|---|---|
| Old McDonald had a farm | E I E I O |
| And on his farm he had some pigs, | E I E I O |

With an oink, oink here,

And an oink, oink there,

Here an oink, there an oink,

Pigs everywhere in sight.

If those pigs get out of line:

PORK AND BEANS TONIGHT!

Old McDonald had a farm,                                      E I E I O

And on his farm he had all these animals,                     E I E I O

    With a chick, chick here,

    And a moo-moo there,

Here an oink, there an oink

    And we're telling you,

If those animals get out of line:

    WE'LL HAVE MULLIGAN STEW!

## STRANGER-DANGER(in SONG and in RHYMING SKIT dialogue

(Tune: Satan Takes a Holiday)

STOP—LOOK—AND LISTEN, MY FRIEND
WE MAY SAVE YOU FROM A TERRIBLE END;
> We mean the Stranger-Danger may be 'round the corner.
> You may meet him going to or from school.

It may be when you're shopping, or when you're babysitting some day.
Stranger-Danger's always looking for a fool.
> He may be any age, he may be young or old,
> Still he is a villain of whom to beware.

He's up to no good, brother, though he may claim to know your mother.
That's the way he lures his victims everywhere.
> WATCH OUT, HE'S COMING OUT,
> WE'LL SHOW YOU WHAT HE'S ALL ABOUT:

## The SKITS:

Little old lady, if you'll go to the bank
Draw out your dough, I'll double your wealth.
> *I warn you, young man, I'm wise to your plan.*
> *Cheating little old ladies may be hazardous to your health.*

Remember, Stranger-Danger could mean trouble for you
Evil is the name of his little game.
Whenever you suspect somebody is bad, don't hesitate to
Call a policeman who'll know what to do.

You want buy some pills or pot, I've got all the things you need,
To take a flight, out of sight, with LSD and SPEED.
> *You can't tempt me with pills and pot, even aspirins give me a pain,*
> *So cool your sidewalk commercial, 'cause your words are all in vain.*
> *I wouldn't care if they were free, 'cause they're all "N.G." to me.*

Congratulations, lovely lady, I bring you gifts galore,
'Tis I, your friendly salesman, will you open up the door?
> *No need to knock upon this door, or try to get your foot in it!*
> *My father's a policeman, and he'll be home any minute!*

Would you like to take a walk with me, to see the latest movie?
I'll buy you everything, you see I think you're really groovy.

*My feet are tired, I've seen the shows, but I haven't finished yet.*
*You can't buy everything you see, because what you see,*
*Is what you don't get!*
How about a ride in a shiny new car, hemmy engine and torsion bar
4-barrel carb and dual exhaust, slicks and mags, that's really boss!
Have you ever seen anything like it, Son?
*Yeah, my father just got rid of one!*

## FERDINAND, THE BULL

Oh, there once lived a bull, a magnificent bull
    In a pasture near old Barcelona.

He would romp and he'd play thru the flowers all day
    Till he'd smell just like O-dee-Colonna.

    He was gentle and kind, and his MOO was refined
    Which the rest of the bulls resented
    For, when he'd start to MOO, in a moment or two,
    He'd have all the cows discontented.

CHORUS:
    Ferdinand, Ferdinand, the bull with the delicate ego.
    Ferdinand, Ferdinand, the heifers all called him "Amigo".
    Ferdinand, Ferdinand, he'd curtsy and greet them politely.
    Now he knew how to tango and dance the fandango,
    But he never learned to fight.

◆    ◆    ◆

## WHISTLE A HAPPY TUNE

Whenever I feel afraid, I hold my head erect
And whistle a happy tune, so no one will suspect, I'm afraid.

While shivering in my shoes, I strike a careless pose
(whistle….) and no one ever know, I'm afraid.

    The result of this deception is very strange to tell,
    For when I fool, the people I fear, I fool myself as well.

I whistle a happy tune, and ev-ry single time
The happiness in the tune convinces me that I'm not afraid.

Make believe you're brave, and the trick will take you far.
You may be as brave as you make believe you are.
     (whistle......)
     (whistle......)

**YOU MAY BE AS BRAVE, AS YOU MAKE BELIEVE YOU ARE!**

## SONNY BOY (Father and Son, vaudeville skit)

### (Father)

When there are gray skies, I don't mind the gray skies,
You make them blue, Sonny Boy.

Friends may forsake me, let them all forsake me,
You'll pull me through, Sonny Boy.

>   You're sent from Heaven, and I know your worth.
>   You made a Heaven, for me, right here on earth.

When I'm old and gray, dear, promise you won't stray, dear
For I love you so, Sonny Boy.

>   (the duet begins):

(Father)(with boy on knee)                     (Son)(licking a giant lollipop)

| (Father)(with boy on knee) | (Son)(licking a giant lollipop) |
|---|---|
| When there are gray skies | Do you like 'em? |
| I don't mind the gray skies, | What do I do, Daddy? |
| You make them blue, | Who am I? |
| Sonny Boy. | |
| | |
| Friends may forsake me, | What'll you do? |
| Let them all forsake me, | What'll I do? |
| You'll pull me through, | What's my name? |
| Sonny Boy. | |

You came from Heaven,

And I know your worth,

You made a Heaven,

For me, right here, on earth

When I'm old and gray, dear,

Promise you won't stray, dear,

For I love you so,

SONNY BOY.

Where did I come from?

How much did I cost?

What did I do?

For who, right where, on what?

GOD BLESS ME!

Then what?

I promise.

What's my name?

## <u>GIVE A LITTLE WHISTLE</u> (and let your conscience be your guide)

(from the movie "Pinocchio)
Give yourself a cross-examination
Are you just about to make a big mistake?
Well, here's a way to save the situation,
So learn it now, for goodness sake.
  Give your better self a break!

When trouble's headed for you, just keep moving right along, and
  Give a little whistle (whistle)
  Give a little whistle (whistle)

When you meet temptation and the urge is very strong,
  Give a little whistle (whistle)
  Give a little whistle (whistle)

Not just a little squeak, pucker up and blow
And, if your whistle's weak, yell

  **STICKS AND STONES MAY BREAK MY BONES
  BUT NAMES WILL NEVER HARM ME.**

Take the straight and narrow path, and if you start to slide,
  Give a little whistle (whistle)
  Give a little whistle (whistle)

**AND ALWAYS LET YOUR CONSCIENCE BE YOUR GUIDE.**

## KEEP THE SPIRIT (Tune: Battle Hymn of the Republic)

(Parody lyrics by: Joan Wellander-Kleppe)

(sing with bell tones)

**DING DONG DING DONG**
**DING DONG DING DONG**

When we hear the bells of Christmas
Ring out sounds of Christmas cheer,
Let us keep the Christmas spirit,
In our hearts each day, all year.

With each act of love and kindness
Fear and hate will disappear.

FOR A PEACEFUL NEW YEAR.

Glory, glory in the highest,
Glory, glory in the highest,
Glory, glory in the highest,
PEACE ON EARTH, GOOD WILL TO MEN.

(2nd verse: a little slower and broader)

Remember, love your neighbor
Is the Golden Rule's command.
Be a little kinder, help him
When he needs a helping hand.

Spread the spirit of true brotherhood
Across this golden land.

TO LOVE YOUR FELLOW MAN.

Glory, glory in the highest,
Glory, glory in the highest,

**Glory, glory in the highest,**
**PEACE ON EARTH, GOOD WILL TO MEN.**

# M-O-T-H-E-R

(1st Chorus)                                   (2nd Chorus)

M—is for the Million things she gave me.       M—is for the Mercy she possesses.

O—means only that she's growing Old.           O—means that I Owe her all I Own.

T—is for the Tears she's shed to save me.      T—is for her Tender sweet caresses.

H—is for her Heart of purest gold.             H—is for her Hands that made a Home.

E—is for her Eyes with lovelight shining.      E—means Everything she's done to help me.

R—means Right, and Right she'll always be.     R—means Real and Regular you see.

> Put them all together, they spell Mother—
> A word that means the world to me.

◆     ◆     ◆

## LET A WINNER LEAD THE WAY

(INTRO:) BUM–BUM BUM—BUM BUM BUM BUM BUM

Will everyone here, kindly step to the rear, and let a winner lead the way.
Here's where we separate the notes from the noise,
> The men from the boys,
> Good sports from the "never try-outs".

Back in the group, we came up with a scoop:
This was the time to rise and say, HIP-HIP HOO-RAY!

> You can't win 'em all, but you try just the same,
> Win or lose, it's how you play the game.

So, everyone here, kindly step to the rear, and let a winner lead the way.

## CECILIA
### (For soft-shoe routine)

(Lyrics divided between the two performances)

1) DOES YOUR MOTHER KNOW YOU'RE OUT, SA-SEEL-YAH
2) Tum  ta  tum  ta  tum  ta  tum,  sa  -seel—yah

1) DOES SHE KNOW THAT I'M ABOUT, SA-SEEL-YAH
2) Tum  ta  tum  ta  tum  ta  ba-ba-ba  ba-ba-ba-bum

1) OH MY, WHEN I, LOOK IN YOUR EYES
2) WHA-WA  WHA-WA  WOW-WOW-WOW-WOW

1) SOMETHING TELLS ME, YOU AND I SHOULD GET TOGETHER, WOW
2) Oo- OOOO,  Oo  OOO,  doo-wacka-doo-wacka-doo-doo-doo-doo-WOW

1) HOW ABOUT A LITTLE KISS, SA-SEEL-YAH
2) How  about  a  little  kiss,    mmmm—yah

1) JUST A KISS YOU'LL NEVER MISS, SA-SEEL-YAH
2) Just  a  kiss  you'll  never  miss,  mmmm—yah

1) WHY DO WE TWO, KEEP ON WASTING TIME
2) Ch  -ch  -ch  -ch    we're  wasting  time

1) OH SA-SEEL-YAH, SAY THAT YOU'LL BE MINE
2) Doodle  dee  -doo  dee  doo  dee  doo  yah

1) OH SA-SEEL-YAH, SAY THAT YOU'LL BE MINE
2) Ba  -ba  ba  ba  ba  ba  ba  bum  yah

## <u>ONE GOD</u>

|                                                        | (ECHO)            |
| ------------------------------------------------------ | ----------------- |
| MILLIONS OF STARS PLACED IN THE SKY BY ONE GOD         | ONE GOD           |
| MILLIONS OF MEN LIFT UP THEIR EYES TO ONE GOD          | ONE GOD           |

    SO MANY CHILDREN CALLING TO HIM
    BY MANY A DIFFERENT NAME,
    ONE FATHER, LOVING EACH THE SAME.

|                                                        |                   |
| ------------------------------------------------------ | ----------------- |
| MANY THE PATHS WINDING THEIR WAY TO ONE GOD            | ONE GOD           |
| MANY THE WAYS ALL OF US PRAY TO ONE GOD               | ONE GOD           |

    WALK WITH ME BROTHER
    THERE WERE NO STRANGERS
    AFTER HIS WORK WAS DONE,

| FOR YOUR GOD    | YOUR GOD    |
| AND MY GOD      | AND MY GOD  |
| ARE ONE.        | ARE ONE.    |

| YOUR GOD        | YOUR GOD    |
| AND MY GOD      | AND MY GOD  |
| ARE ONE.        | ARE ONE.    |

# CHICAGO:I:WILL

-COPYRIGHT 1971-
Lyrics & Music
by
Joan M. Wellander

DEDICATED TO
Chicago—
the "I Will" City

City Hall

City Hall

SOUVENIR EDITION

PREMIER PERFORMANCE

Chicago Police-Fire Thrill Show

August 14-15 - Soldier Field

The 19th District Jr. Patrol Choir, under the direction of Joan Wellander

# CHICAGO: I WILL

*An anthem for the city of Chicago—based on the city's motto, "I Will".*
*Composed by Joan Wellander-Kleppe—Copyright 1970*
*Arranged by Dr. David Thompson*

**INTRODUCTION:**

From the great Chicago Fire, a wonder city grew
Because people then, like now, helped the spirit rise anew.
Yes, that great Chicago spirit which overcomes adversity
Still finds its strength in you and me, and neighborhood diversity.

**CHORUS:**

1. Proudly we claim that our city is second to none—
   The hub of the great Middle West.
   Home of the Loop and Magnificent Mile,
   Her lakefront and parks are the best.

   Chicago works for the good of each great neighborhood
   And proves this is where people care.
   Standing tall, side by side, let your pride rise and shine
   Repeating our motto—it's yours and it's mine:  Chicago, I Will.

2. Proudly we claim that our city is second to none==
   The hub of the great Middle West.
   Home of the Loop and Magnificent Mile,
   Her lakefront and parks are the best.

   Send up a cheer, loud and clear, let our song fill the air,
   Chicago is where people care.
   Join the great civic leaders, you're part of the team
   To prove that our motto fulfills ev'ry dream:  Chicago, I Will.

3.  Proudly we claim that our city is second to none—
    The hub of the great Middle West.
    Home of the Loop and Magnificent Mile,
    Her lakefront and parks are the best.

    Stand up and cheer for the people we love and respect,
    Who gallantly serve and protect.
    Standing tall, side by side, let your loyalty shine.
    Remember our motto, it's yours and it's mine:  Chicago, I Will.

# SOME INTERESTING FACTS ABOUT CHICAGO

INCORPORATED: March 3, 1837
MILES OF LAKEFRONT: 30
PARKS: 7,000 acres

FIRST CITY HALL: Located on southeast corner of Clark and Lake Streets, known as the "Saloon", (synonym for 'Salon' in French) building—then referred to as the largest and most beautiful hall west of Buffalo.

PRESENT CITY HALL: Dedicated February 11, 1911, occupies an entire city block, bounded by Randolph/LaSalle/Clark/Washington streets. The main entrance is flanked by four relief panels in granite, typifying four great features of municipal government: City Playgrounds, Public Schools, the Parks System, and the Water Supply System.

Chicago's motto, "I WILL", expressed in the figure above, is a conception of strength, vitality, and heroism—standing youthful, energetic, and bold—typifying Chicago's character. Its pose suggests the combination of steadfastness and progress that has made Chicago the "Wonder City of the World".

The leathern strap about the wrist is symbolic of such as used by athletes to reinforce the muscles; the carpenter's square signifies the peaceful idea of labor and industry of the era, when, according to scriptural verse, swords shall be beaten into ploughshares, and spears into pruning hooks. The phoe-

nix crest above the broadening brow recalls the seemingly hopeless cata-
clysm, the Chicago Fire, from which the Chicago spirit rose anew.

CHICAGO FLAG: Two blue bars (representing the North and South
branches of the Chicago River) divide the white background fringed in gold,
into three segments (designating the three geographical sections of the city:
north, west, and south sides); the center of which contains four red stars
symbolizing Fort Dearborn (established in 1803, destroyed in 1812); the
Great Chicago Fire of 1871; World's Columbian Exposition of 1893; and
the Century of Progress in 1933-1934. (Chicago police wear a patch of this
design on their uniforms).

CHICAGO SEAL MOTTO: "Urbs in Horto" means "City in a Garden".
CHICAGO FIRE: Sunday, October 8, 1871, destroyed 1/3 of the city, took
300 lives
CHICAGO POLICE DEPARTMENT: Created by ordinance in 1855,
CHICAGO FIRE DEPARTMENT: Created by ordinance in 1858.
SOLDIER FIELD: Commemorates Chicago war dead of World War I.

*The 19th District Patrolboys A Cappella Choir sang at Headquarters under the direction of Joan Wellander.*

# 19th DISTRICT JR. PATROL BOYS CHOIR

## Performs
## at
## POLICE HEADQUARTERS

*Voices of youth lifted in songs of the season at a program in Headquarters lobby.*

### 19th DISTRICT JR. PATROL BOYS CHOIR
### Performs
### at a
### church ice cream social

## ...angel
## voices...

Voices of angels may exist only in the heart, but the closest to them today must be the voices of a well trained boys' choir.

The Town Hall police district boys glee club is one example.

They'll carol at St. Andrew's church, 3546 N. Pauline st., before midnight mass Christmas eve. Meantime, their rehearsals and caroling sessions show all of the enthusiasm displayed at right and the horror of bad amplifier acoustics indicated by boys with hands to their ears below.

CHICAGO TODAY Photos by Lee Otas

### at
### Christmas Eve Midnight Mass
### Saint Andrew Church - Chicago

**19th DISTRICT JR. PATROL BOYS CHOIR**

**Rehearsing**

# CHICAGO POLICE-FIRE
# THRILL SHOW
**Performing**

*Supt. James B. Conlisk, Jr. salutes the colors.*

# CHICAGO POLICE-FIRE THRILL SHOW

*Mayor Richard J. Daley attended the show with his grandchildren accompanied by Col. Jack Reilly, who directs special events for the Mayor's Office.*

# FOLLOW THESE SIMPLE RULES

*(When you're stopped by the police)*

When a police officer pulls up behind you, lights flashing, there are a few procedures to follow:

- As carefully and expeditiously as possible, pull to the right side of the road and onto the shoulder. Come to a complete stop and wait.

- Do not get out of your car. Set and wait for the officer to approach you. It is dangerous for motorists to walk back to the police car because they may be struck by another vehicle. The police would prefer to have you sitting instead of moving around.

- Don't dive for the glove box or go under your seat to get something. That can make a police officer nervous because he has no way of knowing whether the driver is reaching for a wallet or a gun.

- Just pull over and stop. People should know where their license, registration, and insurance card are, so that it doesn't take 20 minutes to get them out.

- Some people think they have 24 hours to bring their license to the police station, but that is not true.

- If it's dark out, motorists may turn on the dome light in their car, allowing the officer to see inside more easily.

- Motorists should keep their hands in plain view on the steering wheel.

- If you need to go into the glove compartment or under the seat, first ask permission.

- Be a good listener. Let the officer explain why you've been stopped, and don't be argumentative. It may be that the officer simply stopped you to let you know that you have a brake light out.

# ABOUT THE AUTHOR

## JOAN WELLANDER-KLEPPE

As a career professional secretary and amateur musician/writer/musical comedy actress, she utilized these qualifications during the five years spent at Chicago's 19th Police District: assisting the District Commander with his innovative 'Junior Patrol' program; founding an a cappella choir; and answering children's letters sent to Officer Friendly "Uncle" George Zaranti.

The excerpts and drawings from children's letters in this collection have not been edited as to spelling and grammar. The children's ages ranged from six to ten years old, representing first-through-fourth graders in Chicago's public, private, and parochial schools. Officer Friendly George Zaranti creatively forged a trust with the thousands of children through his obvious sincerity blended with a refreshing sense of humor.

This and other innovative programs unique to the 19th Police District, such as the Junior Patrol and the Boys A Cappella Choir, were effective in reaching young people with the hope of keeping them focused in the right direction—giving them something positive to belong to, diverting them from joining a gang in the area.

Officer Zaranti involved himself with all of these programs, subliminally filling the children's need for a male role model and projecting a positive image of law enforcement personnel.

# *IN MEMORIAM*

### *SERGEANT WILLARD E. KLEPPE*

| | |
|---|---|
| *Appointed:* | *1952* |
| *Married:* | *1978* |
| *Retired:* | *1985* |
| *Deceased:* | *1988* |

### *PATROLMAN GEORGE ZARANTI:*

| | |
|---|---|
| *Appointed:* | *1964* |
| *Married:* | *1972* |
| *Retired:* | *1992* |
| *Deceased:* | *1994* |

*The unconditional love of children, as shown by these two police officers, inspired the authorship of this book. Coincidentally, both of these men found fulfilling happiness the 'second-time-around', being a loving father, and a husband to a girl named "Joan".*

*Joan Wellander's children—Tom, Alan, Barbara—dearly loved the Sergeant. Joan Zaranti presented Sammy, Angela, and Tony to George with great love.*

978-0-595-40048-5
0-595-40048-5

www.ingramcontent.com/pod-product-compliance
Lightning Source LLC
Chambersburg PA
CBHW051413280526
45785CB00003B/1059